RAISED ON STEAM

The author is just a little wary of Stanier 5XP 4-6-0 No 5614 *Leeward Islands* waiting to leave St Pancras in 1937 with an express for Manchester Central. From a total class of 191 examples, No 5614 was built at Crewe in 1934 and allocated to 14B Kentish Town, where she remained for most of her working life. The platform trolleys are loaded with an assortment of bits and pieces including a good supply of railway tail lamps.

RAISED ON STEAM

The pre-war railway photographs of
Frank Carrier
selected and described by his son
Michael Carrier

Foreword by R. H. N. ('Dick') Hardy

· RAILWAY HERITAGE ·
from
The NOSTALGIA Collection

First published in 2006

British Library Cataloguing in Publication Data

A catalogue record for this book is available from the British Library.

ISBN 1 85794 270 1
ISBN 978 1 85794 270 5

Silver Link Publishing Ltd
The Trundle
Ringstead Road
Great Addington
Kettering
Northants NN14 4BW

Tel/Fax: 01536 330588
email: sales@nostalgiacollection.com
Website: www.nostalgiacollection.com

Printed and bound in Great Britain

SLP

A Silver Link book
from
The NOSTALGIA *Collection*

Below Derby Locomotive Works offices and clock tower form the backdrop as Kirtley '2F' 0-6-0 No 2819, with round-topped boiler and outside frames, stands waiting to go forward to Chaddesden Yard with a train of empty wagons in about 1930. Built at the Vulcan Foundry in 1873, she has received the large extended cab but still retains her number on the tender and 'LMS' on the cab side. She was allocated to Shed 1 Derby when the photograph was taken.

Newly painted, recently outshopped engines from Derby Works stand at various locations in the background.

Opposite page My great interest in railway operating was largely derived from being taken by Dad at an early age to Breadsall Crossing signal box and experiencing the running of a railway at first hand. Signalman Tommy Haines, pictured here, was a dedicated railwayman who took a delight in explaining the workings of the box to a fascinated youngster. Of particular interest at Breadsall Crossing was the large hand-operated wheel inside the box, which was turned to open and close the level crossing gates over the road below. The signal box in operation at that time had opened in 1891 and closed on 13 July 1969 when Derby power box took over the workings and the road ceased to cross the railway.

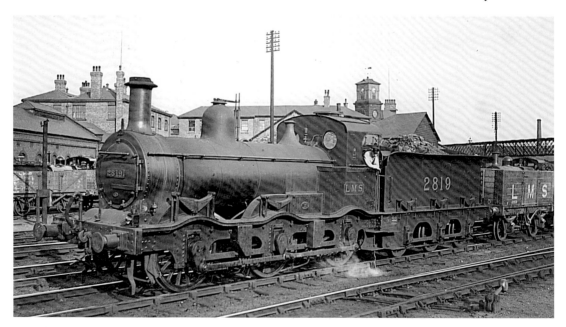

Contents

This is probably the only half-decent shot in the collection of my father Frank Carrier actually on a locomotive! It should immediately be pointed out that the generally dilapidated condition of the engine and the bent handrails were there beforehand and he was in no way responsible...

The section of the main-line railway through Ambergate was widened between 1928 and 1932 and this necessitated the uncovering of the 101-yard Longland Tunnel. The firm of Shanks & McEwan carried out the work and *Bonnie Dundee* was one of the locomotives used in the project.

Foreword

by
R. H. N. ('Dick') Hardy

Mike Carrier and I first met when I was in my last job at BRHQ and he was a down-to-earth and very knowledgeable Operations Assistant to the Area Manager at Carlisle. Unlike his father, who was an extremely able, skilled and practical design engineer in the CME's department at Derby, Mike chose to make his career in the Operating side – indeed, included in this book is some very early pictorial evidence of basic instruction in signalling! Later on he became involved through changes in organisation with locomotive matters and enginemen, and when I heard that he was working on a book of his father's photographs, I knew that the result would be something remarkable. And so it has proved to be.

F. G. Carrier did much of his photography of LMS locomotives and men on the Midland main line and you will find here splendid pictures of the Kirtley, Johnson and Deeley engines and their rebuilds, and you will also see how many alterations were made to the original four-coupled bogie passenger engine of S. W. Johnson's earlier days and how little the basic design was altered even in LMS days. So wherever you look you will be taking a history lesson, but also lessons in operation, while time and again you will be in the presence of the men who actually did the job. Nothing saddens me more than to see page after page of beautiful photographs of steam locomotives without a human being in sight.

There are 'Midland' 'Claughtons' with their GC tenders: there is a marvellous picture of a Webb 'Jumbo' double-heading a rebuilt Caprotti 'Claughton' near Tamworth with the driver of little old No 5011 leaning over the side of the cab and the white feather showing – what a ride he and his fireman would have had, bucking and bouncing along ahead of that big four-cylinder engine! Nearly a hundred years ago, an Oxenholme 'Jumbo' with its own enginemen would go to Carlisle, to Crewe, to Liverpool, to Manchester and home to Windermere with the Club train, all in a 10-hour day – truly men of iron in their little private world. So there is much to see and learn about the Midland and LNWR locomotive scene, but that is only a start.

The LNER – my railway, for I started at Doncaster in January 1941 – also served Derby by way of Friargate station, and there is a photograph of an old GN 'W' in the snow near Breadsall with its train of little old GN coaches, so evocative, for I worked on those 'D2s' in the Works, in the shed and on the road. It also reminds me of the amount of double-heading that the Midland and, in later days, the LMS tolerated, whereas on the M&GN section those same Johnson Class 1 and 2 engines were loaded up to 14-15 Midland bogies single-handed in the summer over the Eastern section to Yarmouth – how they did it over such severe gradients is almost beyond my comprehension, but there you have the steam locomotive, which could, in courageous hands, do what was theoretically quite impossible.

Frank Carrier found two lovely spots on the GN main line to photograph our engines. Inevitably, there are 'Pacifics' roaring out of Grantham with heavy trains to attack Stoke bank – and by the way, how can you tell at a glance whether the 'A1' 'Pacifics' had short-travel valves as built or the long-travel valves that so greatly improved their work? There is GN 'Atlantic' No 4450, climbing up by Saltersford with eight Pullmans, a snip for one of these marvellous engines, and an example of an engine dear to my heart, Class 'B4' No 6099 of Copley Hill shed, with a day excursion from Leeds to King's Cross. They were a part of the West Riding scene for near enough 25 years, and those London jobs were often heavy and hard work.

But we have still barely started, for it is when you come into the world of the colliery and industrial railways that you will be delving deep into history. I never knew that a Brighton 'Rooter', one of a class built in the early 1870s to handle the South London line passenger traffic, would be working at a Derbyshire colliery in the mid-1930s, still with its original type of boiler and Stroudley copper-capped chimney. I knew that the Northumberland and Durham coalfields were served by an amazing variety of historical engines, but never that a Stephen Lewin engine with a species of Worsdell chimney survived there until 1966. There are relics from the Met made redundant by electrification but sold as late as 1927, a Brighton 'E1' tank at work at Cannock, and old North Eastern long-boiler engines, ideal for heavy colliery work, as were the locomotives specially built for the collieries way back in the 19th century. And there are old Mersey engines that had trundled their rough little coaches down and up the 1 in 27 under the famous river and, for light relief, had hauled, no doubt from Rock Ferry, the through Continental service from Folkestone, which arrived at Liverpool Low Level at the beginning of the morning rush-hour back in 1898. Oh, if only old *Cecil Raikes* could talk!

We have the LMS 'Turbo', and there may just be

Edge Hill men who read this book who had the doubtful pleasure of firing No 6202 to Driver Laurie Earl of Camden. When worked hard she burned coal like chaff, and time and again Laurie Earl's fireman would refuse to lodge and would go home passenger so that an Edge Hill Extra Link fireman would have to cope with the activities of that famous, smiling but merciless little driver back to Euston. And there is the Ljungström turbo-condensing engine approaching Derby, no doubt in charge of Driver W. E. Poole of Derby, whom Frank Carrier is bound to have known. She vanished pretty quickly from the scene, but not before Cecil J. Allen travelled behind her and recorded her work for posterity in the July 1927 *Railway Magazine*, page 18.

So I promise you that you will find this book truly interesting and utterly absorbing, and you will come back for more, time and again. The standard of photography is as high as that of the great names of the pre-war scene, and each picture is the work of an understanding, knowledgeable, artistic and very human locomotive engineer, and thankfully given to us by Michael Carrier, who was – and still is, come to that – a railwayman through and through.

A platelayer seems quite content to be part of the photograph as 'A1' No 4473 *Solario* leaves Stoke Tunnel in the early 1930s. No 4473 was one of the early Gresley 'Pacifics' with the 180lb boiler built at

Doncaster immediately after the grouping in 1923. She is seen with the larger GN chimney and the high cab roof fitted to these earlier engines of the class.

Introduction

Apart from his family, the two most important things in Dad's life were steam engines and photography. As a professional railwayman he made the most of his knowledge and his travel facilities to pursue these most worthwhile hobbies. Literally thousands of hours were spent in the evening and at weekends visiting some of his favourite haunts to capture on film steam in its heyday.

Keenly interested in everything that's going on – or just nosey. At an early age the author sits in the driver's seat of an ex-GNR right-hand-drive 'K2' Class 2-6-0 on the West Highland line.

Dad was born into a railway family. My grandfather, Dad's father, was a railwayman at Bedford, then Sheffield, before entering the staff office on the Midland Railway at Derby. Brother Don was a railwayman at Derby too.

Born at the turn of the century, Dad joined the Midland Railway at Derby having served in the Grenadier Guards during the First World War. Through the locomotive works and on the footplate he gained a remarkable insight into steam engine construction and working. He then entered the locomotive Drawing Office under Henry Fowler, and subsequently under many of the LMS and BR Chief Mechanical and Electrical Engineers.

From time to time a certain amount of poetic licence was allowed in the locomotive drawing office. The sight of one of Bulleid's dreadful-looking 0-6-0s built for the Southern Railway prompted this masterpiece! Remarkably, he could knock up something like this in a very short time and took great delight in doing so. The end result would grace the cover of the menu for the office Christmas dinner. The original is framed and held by his grandson, David.

He was a gifted draughtsman and locomotive designer, but the other side of his character saw his astonishing ability to capture the railway in general and the steam engine in particular on film, and he became an important part of an elite 'gang' of enthusiasts. This book poignantly evokes those wonderfully happy days.

I vividly remember as a boy growing up in an atmosphere of railway talk. Many people visited the house to discuss aspects of steam engine working and photography, and it was not surprising that under Dad's enthusiasm and guidance I too became a railwayman, albeit on the operating rather than on the locomotive side. In all I completed 40 years of railway service and witnessed at first hand the change from steam to diesel, then to electrification. Dad did not live to be part of this change, and his beloved steam engine still reigned supreme when he died.

He was an inspiration and he very much moulded my own life to a love and association with the railway industry. This book is dedicated to his love for his family, his work as a professional railwayman and his expertise as a railway photographer.

In conclusion, may I sincerely thank a number of people without whose help this book would not have been possible. First, my Mum, who was often taken to obscure lineside locations and sat for hours while Dad waited patiently for the right 'shot' to come along, also providing endless meals and cups of teas as friends talked railways well into the small hours; to my own wife Ann, who without complaint has patiently given me the encouragement to press on with this venture; to the late Norman Roycroft of Crewe, who has given advice and much encouragement; to Geoff Sheldon and his wife, of Belper, who have spent many, many hours helping me with the photographic side of the book, and looked after me during my many visits to their house; to Jackie Moffat from Ainstable, Cumbria, who has typed it all up for me and helped tremendously in numerous other ways; to both Dick Hardy and Jim Jarvis for their valuable and very much appreciated contributions; and finally, of course, to Peter Townsend and Will Adams of Silver Link Publishing, who have both shared my vision and enthusiasm for publishing Dad's photographs in this book.

I sincerely hope this book gives pleasure and provides interest to all who read it.

Michael Carrier
Armathwaite, Cumbria

Frank Carrier: a recollection

It was my privilege and pleasure to have known Frank Carrier both at work and 'play'. I first met him when I was a boy and my brother Ron invited him and his wife Nan to visit our family house at Harpenden for the weekend in the early 1930s.

Ron, during his brief spell in the Locomotive Drawing Office at Derby, had developed a close friendship with Frank, no doubt partly because of their common interest in locomotives and photography. I recall that it was Frank who aroused Ron's interest in the fascinating array of venerable steam locomotives working in industry, and he also persuaded Ron to use glass plate for his photography work. As a result of this friendship they both went on 'hunting' expeditions in the evening and at weekends to numerous locations to take top-quality portraits of locomotives and trains.

At the onset of the Second World War I followed in Ron's footsteps and started my Engineering Apprenticeship in Derby Locomotive Works. On many evenings we walked the 2 miles from our 'digs' to Frank's home in Allestree for a good chat about engines and technical matters before returning home in the gloom of the blackout – unless there was a full moon!

At the end of the war, myself and Frank, and sometimes his son Michael, made short visits to Breadsall Crossing below Allestree, or to collieries around Ilkeston, together with SLS visits to York and Doncaster.

So much for the 'play'! Let's move on to Frank's professional career. He was born in 1900 (let's not argue whether that was the end or the start of a century!). On leaving school he served in the Grenadier Guards during the latter part of the First World War and, when that was over, the Locomotive Works at Derby.

During that time Frank won the prestigious Sir Henry Fowler Scholarship. Through the works he covered all the various sections and workshops and gained an in-depth working knowledge of the steam engine, including the experience of lengthy spells on the footplate.

In 1924 he entered the Locomotive Drawing Office at Derby located below the clock tower, over the works main offices. The Chief Draughtsman at that time was Herbert Chambers, and shortly afterwards the drawing office moved to new premises in London Road. Frank was a very fast worker on the board and an excellent designer, even though the LMS called such valuable servants merely 'draughtsmen'.

During the Second World War Frank, together with his very capable colleague Ted Fox, quickly worked up schemes for the Riddles 'Austerity' 2-8-0 and 2-10-0 designs. Also, about the same time, Frank almost single-handedly designed the 5ft 3in-gauge 2-6-4 tanks for the NCC in Ireland. Although many features had been used on the Fowler 2-6-4 tanks for the LMS and the NCC 2-6-0s, a considerable number of new drawings were needed and, furthermore, all the common components had to be identified and marked up on existing drawings and sheets prepared for ordering materials. Frank completed that project in one year – an incredible performance by any standard.

In 1942 I entered the same office as Frank when I was loaned during my apprenticeship to colour up a set of general arrangement drawings for the streamlined 'Coronation' 'Pacifics' to be presented to the Derby Technical College. As a distraction from the routine pressures of the drawing office during some of the tea breaks, Frank would rustle up a cartoon sketch of some improbable locomotive and take it along to my 'paintshop' to get its livery. Frank was a real artist and his cartoons used on menu cards for the various office parties became legendary over many years.

After the war the LMS initiated a project to design and build the first large main-line diesel-electric locomotive. I returned to London Road in 1946 and joined a small select Development Office, which comprised Eric Langridge, Ted Fox and Frank. The design work for what was to become No 10000 was a priority and we

BARRER HAMMERTIGHT

STEW SHARPOT

One of the delightful drawings knocked up by Dad during his lunch break. In this case the drawing depicts with remarkable similarity an 0-4-0 built by Sharp Stewart for the Barrow Haematite Iron Works.

undertook the initial scheming, and also the detail design of the bogies.

Also about this time the LMS agreed to pursue Col Fell's scheme for a unique multi-engined gearbox-drive locomotive, and Frank was deputed to scheme out this new locomotive in conjunction with Col Fell. It has been said that Fell reckoned that Frank was one of the best designers he had met, and that was praise indeed from a top Rolls Royce engineer. Frank's desk was immediately behind mine and, from a clean sheet of paper first thing, by lunchtime a completely new and complicated drawing was finished.

Soon after nationalisation, after I had been promoted elsewhere, Frank became heavily involved in preparing diagrams for the proposed BR Standard steam locos to E. S. Cox's requirements. In most cases the actual initial work that Frank undertook closely represented the actual locomotives as built.

Late in 1951 Frank was rushed into Derby Infirmary for an operation and remained very ill for some months before returning home. On my return from a two-year stay in the USA in September 1952 I was anxious to talk to him about my trip and show him my colour slides, but sadly he had, by then, returned to hospital.

When I visited him there it was a traumatic experience to see him so ill, and it was not long before he passed away at the early age of 52.

He will always be remembered as both a staunch friend and a good colleague.

Jim Jarvis
Harpenden

1. Derby and south

Crossing the complex London Road Junction immediately south of Derby station in late 1927 is an up Manchester Central to St Pancras express hauled by Johnson 4-2-2 'Single' No 644 piloting a Midland Compound. In the background are the station buildings, and to the right is part of the long footbridge that led from the street into the locomotive works. Engine Shed Sidings No 2 signal box is also clearly visible.

No 644 was built at Derby in 1893 with a single pair of 7ft 6½in driving wheels. She was one of a class of 95 locomotives of five variations. Introduction of the steam sanding apparatus made single-wheelers a more practical proposition when considering the more moderate train loads of that day, but all had gone by 1928, except for No 673, which was repainted, renumbered and ultimately preserved.

Above The roof of London Road Junction signal box is just visible on the extreme left as the coaching stock of No 67 special is worked away to the carriage sidings from Derby station in 1927. The locomotive is Midland 4-4-0 No 442; built by Johnson at Derby in 1894, she retains her round-topped boiler, number on the tender and the LMS coat of arms on the splashers. The leading vehicle is an ex-Midland non-vestibule Brake, and on the right the landmark feature is the notable water tower on long cast-iron legs.

Below At the north end of Derby station in 1925 a pair of early Johnson 4-4-0s await departure from Platform 1 with a Manchester Central express. The picture shows the fine overall roof of the station, long since removed, and also the clock tower and part of the buildings and offices of the locomotive works on the extreme left. The leading engine, No 398, was built at Derby in 1891; she retains the round-topped boiler, Midland coat of arms on the splasher and 'MR' on the front buffer-beam. When the photograph was taken she was allocated to Shed 21 – Trafford Park (Manchester).

Experiments with steam engines were constantly being made in efforts to improve efficiency – in particular steaming capabilities – and to reduce the amount of coal and water used. The then CME of the LMS, Henry Fowler, was intrigued by a proposal to build an engine using steam turbine technology, and such an engine was built at Beyer Peacock in 1927, and known as the Ljungström turbo-condensing engine.

With his railway connections, Dad was aware of the use of this unusual engine on revenue-earning expresses from Manchester Central, and took advantage of this by photographing the engine approaching Derby station from the north. Following the trials, the LMS was not impressed and the locomotive was returned to its makers later in the year.

Still of lower-quadrant pattern, the Midland signals to the right of the engine are on the lines to Spondon via Chaddesden Yard.

Above Resplendent in red, Johnson No 201, retaining its round-topped boiler, sits at the north end of Derby station in 1930. This 2-4-0, designed by Johnson, dates from 1876 and was the first main-line passenger engine for the Midland Railway. The class comprised engines of four driving wheel sizes, and No 201, from Shed 1 Derby, was one of those with 7ft 0in examples.

Behind the engine is Engine Shed Sidings No 1 signal box, opened in 1892 and finally closed in July 1969, and part of the signalling workshops.

Below Brand new three-cylinder 'Baby Scot' 5XP 4-6-0 No 5954 waits to leave Derby shed on 25 March 1933 to work an express south. She had been delivered to traffic just a few days beforehand, one of a class of 52 engines. In 1937 she became No 5520 and was named *Llandudno*. Piles of good steam coal can be seen neatly stacked in the shed yard. The lower-quadrant signals belong to London Road Junction.

Built for working over tight-radius curves in breweries and other works yards, 28 engines of this Johnson 0-4-0 class were built between 1883 and 1900. Four survived to nationalisation and the last one was withdrawn in 1958. No 1509 was Derby-built in 1897 and has acquired a stove-pipe chimney. In the second view the driver and fireman pose happily enough at Litchurch Lane, Derby, before their next shunting duty in the nearby locomotive works.

Interest in producing steam at very high pressure resulted in the LMS ordering a 'Royal Scot' 4-6-0 from the North British Locomotive Company with a high-pressure boiler. The result was No 6399 *Fury*, fired up for the first time on 6 December 1929. She was delivered to Polmadie shed in January 1930 for trials, but regrettably, in the following month when on a test run to Carstairs, a tube in the high-pressure boiler burst, resulting in a footplate crew fatality.

No 6399 was repaired and delivered to Derby in 1932, where tests were carried out in the years to 1934, interrupted by two serious failures. Following the problems, a decision was taken to rebuild the engine, and in 1935 *Fury* became No 6170 *British Legion*, and the concept of high-pressure locomotives died. The rebuilding of the engine with a taper boiler and larger cylinders meant that she became the prototype for the subsequent rebuilding of the whole 'Royal Scot' Class.

Above This quite remarkable engine was built at Derby in 1919 specifically for the task of banking trains up the 1 in 37 Lickey Incline. No 2290 (later 22290 as photographed) was always unofficially known as 'Big Bertha'. She had four cylinders and a tractive effort of 43,313lb, and latterly was fitted with an electric headlamp to assist drivers when going up behind standing trains in the dark. Due to the short distances involved in her task, she had a relatively small tender, but the nature of the work necessitated an overhaul at Derby Works every 11 months or so.

Below This post-war shot shows an engine with which Dad had much involvement. Not the most handsome of locomotives, the LMS standard 4F 2-6-0s were fitted with a high running plate, external regulator rod, and cylinders and motion all designed to ease maintenance in the difficult period for steam following the Second World War. No 3000 was built at Horwich in 1947 and photographed at Derby soon afterwards. Together with four sister engines (Nos 3001-4) she was allocated to Crewe South when new, but later spent some time at Rowsley before returning to the Western Division of the LMS.

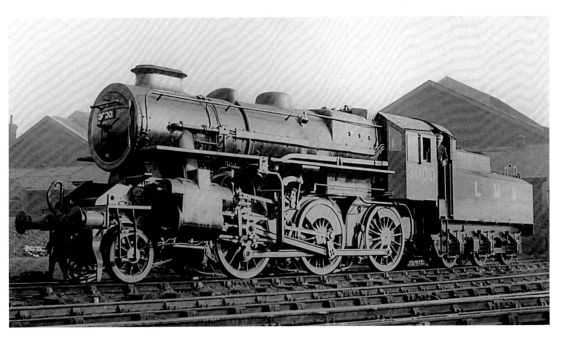

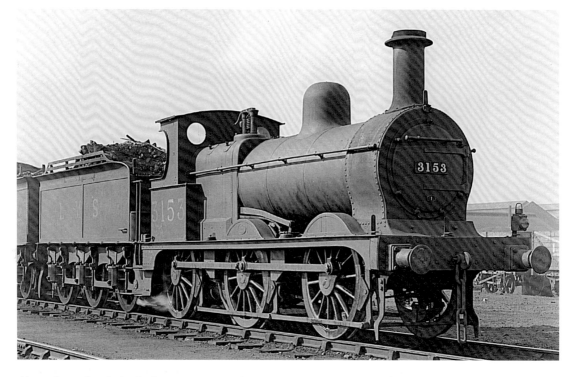

Above It was handy for Dad to pop over to 4 Shed at Derby to photograph an array of engines either allocated there or, in many cases, running in after overhaul in the workshops. These next four photographs try to do justice to a location ever full of change and interest.

On 5 May 1934 Johnson 2F 0-6-0 No 3153 is coaled up and ready to take up its next working. Built at Derby in 1886, she retains the short cab but has been rebuilt with a Belpaire boiler. An engine from an enormous class of 976 examples built between 1875 and 1908, she was allocated to Shed 1 Derby in 1934.

Below Looking smart with large numbers on the cab side, this photograph of No 3603 was taken at Derby on the same day. Driver and fireman pose, seemingly quite proud of their mount, before taking her off the shed for the next job. This 0-6-0 was built at Neilson's in 1899 and has a large cab as well as a Belpaire boiler.

Above Originally Midland Railway No 341, LMS No 22822 was built at the Vulcan Foundry in 1873 and rebuilt in 1908 and 1922. Looking smart, having been recently overhauled and painted, she has been rebuilt with a Belpaire boiler but still retains the outside frames on the engine and tender. Four of the class survived until BR days, and No 22822, allocated to Burton-on-Trent for many years, was one of those, finally being withdrawn in 1949.

Below On 5 May 1934 Johnson 2P 4-4-0 No 402 stands proudly on the shed at Derby. Built in 1891 and rebuilt in 1922, she was allocated to Shed 25 Sheffield Millhouses.

As far as is known this is the only picture in existence of a Garratt working a train comprised totally of passenger vehicles. In 1936 LMS Derby experimented by arranging a special in passenger train timings using No 4999, one of the three Garratts fitted with vacuum brakes. Dad was 'in the know' and went to Borrowash to photograph the event, while the official railway photographers went to Sharnbrook to film the engine on the climb there. The train, consisting of 20 passenger vehicles, with the Dynamometer Car next to the engine and all wired up, left Derby for St Pancras, but in the event No 4999 suffered a hot axle box and had to be taken off at Leicester. The experiment was not repeated.

Three Garratts were built at Beyer Peacock in 1927, followed by 30 more in 1930. Built for the Toton-Wellingborough-Brent coal traffic, they did sterling work for more than 25 years. However, they were extremely heavy on maintenance and were all withdrawn and broken up between 1955 and 1958.

The Derby Riverlands scheme arose from the need to straighten the River Derwent south of Derby following the disastrous floods of 1932. A 3ft 0in-gauge railway was laid in order to transport materials around the site, and 11 engines, including two Sentinels, were brought in to provide the motive power. After the work was completed the engines were sold and moved on. One such engine, *Hodder*, similar to *Fylde*, was built by Peckett's of Bristol and, after conversion and re-gauging, worked for many years on the Crich Railway near Ambergate.

Three examples of the engines used on the Riverlands scheme were photographed near Alvaston on 12 July 1933. *Riverlands Dora* was the sister engine to *Gwen*, both being built by Bagnall of Stafford in 1904, works numbers 1682 and 1683. At some stage in her working life *Riverlands Dora* obtained a stovepipe chimney, but *Gwen* retained her original. *Fylde* was another 0-4-0 tank built by Peckett, this time in 1924, to works number 1671. The wagons are good examples of the simple construction of vehicles used on small narrow gauge railways at that time.

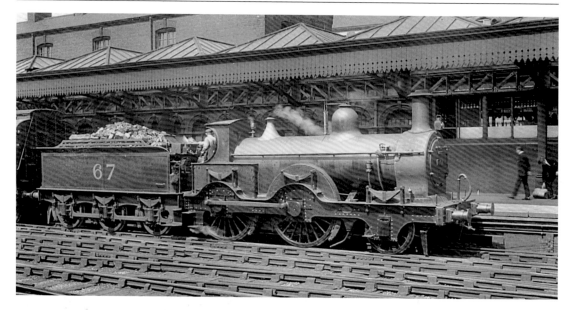

Above A good place to see the trains of two completely different railways was Nottingham Midland station. Over the top ran the Great Central main line on a large iron bridge, and it was quite easy to see the engines and trains as they rattled overhead, although photography was virtually impossible.

However, down below the Midland station was busy enough with a constant passage of both freight and passenger trains. These three pictures depict the scene. The first is an early picture taken around 1928 showing Kirtley 2-4-0 No 67 on a Nottingham to Leicester local stopping train. No 67 was built at Derby in 1870, and was unlikely to have been altered much

since, retaining the outside frames, round-topped boiler and small cab. She was of the Midland '800' Class, of which there were 48 examples. All had been withdrawn by 1928 except for No 60 (later 20060), which survived until 1936.

Below No 275 is a Johnson engine built in 1881. There were four varieties of the class, depending on the size of the driving wheel; in the case of 275 this was 7ft 0in. It is likely that she has arrived from the Seaton or Stamford areas, having an LNWR non-corridor carriage next the engine. The billboards and enamel signs on the platform would make interesting reading today.

Above No 747 is a Midland 3P 4-4-0 built by Johnson at Derby in 1904. This class was the first on the Midland Railway to be built with a Belpaire-firebox boilers. She was superheated in 1924, and this view, taken in 1925, shows the engine with its number on the tender and LMS coat of arms on the cab sides.

Above The earliest of these three Midland Railway 2-4-0 passenger engines, No 20012, was built by Kirtley at Derby in 1869. She was from a class of 22 engines, many of which were long-lived, the last one not being withdrawn until 1947. Seen at Kettering in 1934, she was allocated to Shed 12 there.

Below No 20060 was from a batch of 48 engines of the '800' Class built by Kirtley in 1870/71; 30 were built by Neilson, the remainder at Derby. They were extremely capable engines and spent many years on main-line working, then latterly piloting heavy expresses until their withdrawal in 1928. However, No 20060 outlived them all, remaining in service until 1936. This photograph was taken at Peterborough East in 1932.

Above No 266 is the youngest of the three, being a Johnson engine built at Derby in 1876 with 6ft 9in driving wheels. She is on her home shed of Kettering (Shed 12) in 1932.

Below No 27217 was an interesting engine. Built by Sharp Stewart in 1858 as an 0-4-0 tank for the London & North Western Railway, she was rebuilt by Adams in 1872 for the North London Railway as an 0-4-2 tank

and had the crane added. She was the permanent shunting engine at Bow Works in East London until withdrawal in 1951.

On the extreme right is one of the London, Tilbury & Southend engines built by Fowler in 1923, based on an earlier Whitelegg design. Numbered 2117, she sports one of the large destination boards so much a feature of LT&S operating. She was also the last locomotive released to service from Derby Works in the old Midland livery and the MR coat-of-arms.

2. Derbyshire

Above The mixed-traffic engines affectionately known as the Horwich 'Crabs' were extremely versatile and reliable locomotives. In all, 245 were built and did sterling work over much of the LMS system. Here No 13055 (later 2755) is seen just north of St Mary's Junction after leaving Derby on a wintry Sunday morning in February 1933. She is at the head of a special 11.00am Derby to Liverpool train, reporting number 72.

Above right The Great Northern Railway line from Derby Friargate to Nottingham Victoria crossed over the Midland main line and climbed through Breadsall GN station to Morley Tunnel. On 12 February 1933

Ivatt Class 'D2' 4-4-0 No 3044 heads a rake of Great Northern articulated stock through the snow on the climb with the 11.30am Derby to Nottingham stopping train.

Right While it was frequent operating practice on the Great Western, it was unusual for the larger locomotive to be the leading engine when double-heading on the LMS. However, on a summer evening in the spring of 1934 a small-boilered 'Claughton' with a Robinson ROD tender leads a Midland 2P 4-4-0 on a down express approaching Breadsall Crossing. A total of 130 four-cylinder 'Claughtons' were built between 1913 and 1921.

Breadsall Crossing signal box's oil hut and signal gantry add much to the scene as Johnson '483' Class 4-4-0 No 443 heads past the box in 1932 with the Paignton to Bradford 'Devonian', and with Great Western vehicles in the formation. No 443 was built in 1894 and rebuilt by Fowler in 1915.

The signal gantry shows the two distant signals (first and third from the left in the picture) applying to the Ripley branch, which left the Midland main line at Little Eaton Junction some three-quarters of a mile to the north. The signals are off on the goods line for a double-headed down freight hauled by a pair of Midland 2F 0-6-0s.

Passing the same spot, LMS Compound No 1098, painted red, makes a fine sight as it passes Breadsall Crossing with the 2.25pm St Pancras to Manchester Central train on 10 August 1934. The leading vehicle is an ex-LNWR 57-foot Corridor Brake Composite. Of interest too are the backs of the distant signal arms: following earlier practice they are square to the arm ends, while later they became chevrons and followed the contour of the signal arm.

Above left These three photographs were taken from the Derby side of Peckwash Mill Sidings signal box on the Midland main line to the north. Clearly seen are the Peckwash Mill down distant signals and the signal wires running to them. The signal box was opened in 1877 and provided rail access to Tempest's Peckwash paper mill; the siding left the up side of the main line and gained entry to the mill by a wooden bridge over the River Derwent. The siding closed in the early part of the century and the paper mill ceased production in 1906.

This was a location for taking late-afternoon or evening photographs when the sun had come far enough round to provide good light on the engine and train. In the first picture a Spondon to Darley Dale local stopping train is hauled by Johnson 2-4-0 No 238 on a late winter evening in 1932. This engine came from a batch of 65 built to Johnson's design of 1876

with 6ft 9in driving wheels. Many were rebuilt in the 1920s with Belpaire boilers and Ramsbottom safety valves. The last Midland 2-4-0 ran until late into 1950.

Left Hughes 2-6-0 No 13095 works hard after leaving Derby with a down special, reporting number 645, on a summer evening in 1934. The engine must have looked resplendent in LMS red with the number in big numerals on the tender and the LMS coat of arms on the cab side.

Above Johnson 2P 4-4-0 No 338 heads a relief St Pancras to Manchester Central express approaching Peckwash Mill in the early 1930s. The vehicle next to the engine is an ex-LNWR 57-foot Corridor Composite still in that company's livery. No 338 was built at Derby in 1882 and subsequently rebuilt with a superheater, Belpaire boiler and extended smokebox.

Above Each of the following four photographs was taken at the same location between Peckwash and Duffield Junction. In the background are Peckwash Mill starting signals, and beneath them Duffield Junction's distants. On the extreme right of the group is the splitting distant for the Wirksworth branch, which left the Midland main line at Duffield Junction. At this point the second down line was classed as 'slow line', which permitted the running of passenger trains as normal practice. During the interval between the late 1920s and the mid-1930s, ie the period between the first and second pair of photographs, the signals were changed from lower-quadrant types to upper-

quadrant in accordance with the new LMS signalling requirements based on the recommendations of the Institute of Railway Signalling Engineers.

In the first photograph a down local stopping train on the 'slow line' is double-headed by No 306, one of the original Johnson 4-4-0s built in 1876 with 6ft 6in driving wheels; 20 more were built the following year with 7ft 0in driving wheels. When this photograph was taken in the late 1920s, No 306 retained the round-topped firebox and spring balance safety valve in the dome. She was withdrawn from service shortly afterwards.

Below left This fine shot of two Kirtley 0-6-0s on a down freight was taken in the late 1920s; both locomotives retain their outside frames on engine and tender. Between 1863 and 1874 several hundred of these were built and most lasted into LMS days, but by 1934 only 20 remained, and the last remained in service until 1951. As was usual at the time, the engine number was on the tender; No 2430 is leading.

Above By the time the 'Royal Scots' had taken over much of the express passenger work on the LNWR main line, Bowen-Cooke four-cylinder 4-6-0

'Claughtons' could be found hard at work on the Midland. Its days already numbered, un-named No 5984 with Robinson ROD tender is seen approaching Duffield Junction with a down express. Of the total of 130 'Claughtons' built between 1913 and 1921, all the small-boilered examples had gone by 1935.

Below Another fine view of a Kirtley 0-6-0 2F hard at work: No 2498 approaches Duffield with an empty wagon train in the early 1930s. Some of the higher-sided wagons were specifically for coke traffic – being lighter in weight, a greater quantity could be conveyed.

These two views show up trains leaving Milford Tunnel on the Midland main line north of Derby. Milford Tunnel signal box controlled the layout at the south end of the tunnel, where two tracks became four; it was opened in 1897 and closed in 1956. Over the tunnel top, exactly on the alignment of the railway, there still remains a four-storey tower built by the North Midland Railway company in 1840; it has been suggested by some authorities that its purpose was to act as a semaphore tower to indicate to drivers of trains using the tunnel whether or not the line was clear. Others suggest it was used by the civil engineer to house optical instruments to accurately plot the course of the railway through the tunnel below. Either way, although now derelict, it was at one time used as a dwelling house.

The first picture, from the early 1930s, shows an up express with reporting

number 628 on both locomotives. The leading locomotive is Johnson 2P 4-4-0 No 350 built at Derby in 1883, piloting Johnson 3P 4-4-0 No 741, built Derby in 1903. Wisps of steam from the safety valves indicate that both engines are steaming well. The train is comprised of ex-Midland stock, including a clerestory vehicle.

At the same location nearly 20 years later, the demand for timber during the

Second World War had substantially altered the background landscape. Kentish Town Class 5 4-6-0 No 4981 heads an up Manchester to Derby local in 1949. Note the sighting-boards behind the two signal arms, designed to give drivers a better view of the signals when the background was diffused, in this case an overbridge.

Above Even well into LMS days, double-heading was very much a feature of Midland Railway working, and here provides a fine sight as Johnson 2P 4-4-0 No 338 leads LMS Compound No 1050 on a down express passing Duffield in 1936. The trees on the left are on the site of Sir Arthur Heywood's famous Duffield Bank Railway.

Below Water in the fields behind the train dates this photograph as 1932, the year of the severe flooding in and around Derby when the River Derwent burst its banks. The signalman in Duffield Junction signal box is attentive to the passage of LMS Compound No 1196, built at the Vulcan Foundry in 1927, on a down St Pancras to Manchester express. The Wirksworth branch and protecting signals can be seen on the right of the picture, and on the left a reminder of the days when milk was conveyed by rail in metal churns. Duffield Junction signal box was opened in 1897, extended in 1910 and finally closed in August 1969.

Above No high-visibility vests insisted upon in those days! A watchful platelayer notes the emergence of LMS Compound No 934 from the southern portal of Milford Tunnel. Photographed in the early 1930s, the train is an up West of England express, and No 934 is allocated to Shed 7 Gloucester. The locomotive was built at the Vulcan Foundry in 1927 and became the last Compound to retain its LMS crimson livery. She was a Derby engine when withdrawn.

Below The following six photographs were taken at one of Dad's favourite locations – the north end of Milford Tunnel. In this north-facing cutting, the actual tunnel mouth sees no sunshine whatsoever, but the

cutting does receive a limited amount of the sun's oblique rays at certain time and seasons; most photographs were taken in the early morning or late evening.

The tunnel was built on the insistence of the landowners, the Strutts of Belper, who demanded that the railway should go through a tunnel rather than interfere with their cotton mill complex, situated within the constraints of a very narrow section of the Derwent valley.

In the first picture LMS Compound No 1050, allocated to Kentish Town, brings a St Pancras to Manchester express out of the unusual tunnel portal in the early 1930s.

Above The tall-chimneyed platelayers' cabin provides a delightful backdrop to Midland Class 3P 4-4-0 No 767 as she leaves the tunnel with a down local stopping train. Originally of the Midland '2606' Class, No 767 was built in 1907 and was from a class of 80 engines that were the first to be built for that company with Belpaire boilers; 22 of the class passed into BR hands in 1948 and the last, No 726, was not withdrawn until 1952. Next to the tender is a Midland Railway horsebox followed by a rake of non-corridor clerestories.

Left From the same '2606' Class, No 776 heads a down express a few hundred yards to the north of Milford Tunnel. Like No 767, the engine is fitted with bogie brakes and, as an experiment in an attempt to improve steaming, has the enlarged Kylala chimney and blastpipe.

Above Obviously on a special working, ex-LNWR 19-inch Goods 4-6-0 No 8813 provides unusual motive power on a train of interesting rolling-stock. No 8813 was allocated at the time to Springs Branch (Wigan), and was one of 170 mixed-traffic inside-cylinder 4-6-0s built by Whale for the LNWR between 1906 and 1909. Just three survived into nationalisation and the final withdrawal was in 1950. The previously mentioned tower above the tunnel can be seen on the hill in the left distance.

Below The next three shots show engines from the numerous ex-Midland Railway 2F 0-6-0 family, of which 976 were built in the 30 years from 1875. The pictures were taken once again at the north end of Milford Tunnel, and while from the same class, each engine is different as the process of rebuilding becomes apparent. In the first photograph No 2950 emerges from the tunnel with a down mixed freight in the early 1930s. While the engine has been rebuilt with inside frames, large cab and Belpaire boiler, the tender is the original, retaining the outside frames.

With a high-sided coke wagon next to the tender, No 3021, built by Dubs in 1878, has clearly filled the tunnel with smoke and emerges into the daylight working hard with a down empty wagon train. Since being built, No 3021 has undergone rebuilds as shown by the extended large cab, inside frames and Belpaire boiler. The tender is now of standard inside-frame design.

Above The final of this trio of 0-6-0s, No 3382 has obtained an inside-framed high-sided tender, but the engine still retains the round-topped boiler and Salter spring balance safety valves on the dome.

Right The wooden platform and gas lamps add to the scene as a young admirer – the author in his early days – closely watches Stanier 5XP 4-6-0 No 5610 *Gold Coast* as she hurries a St Pancras to Manchester express through Ambergate in late 1937. No 5610 was built at Crewe in 1934 and is seen here with the unusual flat high-sided tender fitted to this engine.

Above Slightly further north on the main line to Manchester the railway swings north then west towards Whatstandwell and allows the evening sun to highlight the graceful lines of LMS 2P 4-4-0 No 506 and LMS Compound No 1085 as they double-head the 2.25pm train from St Pancras in the mid-1930s. This must have been a tremendous sight as both engines were painted in maroon with large numbers on the tenders and the LMS coat of arms on each cab side.

Above right These two shots are of up freights on the Midland main line between Whatstandwell and Cromford, where railway, road, canal and river all run together through the valley of the Derwent. The tall chimney in the background belonged to the Ilkeston & Heanor Waterworks, which processed water for supply to those rapidly growing towns. This operation still continues, though the chimney itself has long been pulled down. In the first photograph Kirtley 0-6-0 No 2592 presents a fine sight as she labours with an up Rowsley to Westhouses freight in about 1932. No 2592 was built by Dubs & Co in 1869, and is still very much in the condition in which she was originally built.

Right With High Peak Junction signal box in the distance and the waterworks chimney as background, Midland Railway 4F 0-6-0 No 3966, allocated to Shed 23 Hasland, storms south with an up mixed freight from Rowsley. No 3966 was originally a Midland engine, having been built by Armstrong Whitworth in 1921.

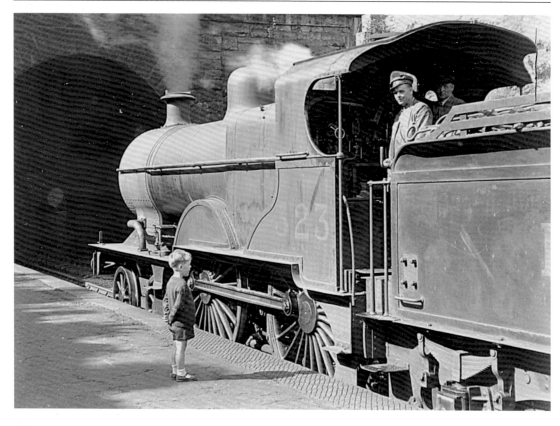

Above The entrance to the 763-yard-long Willersley Tunnel beckons to a Derby to Manchester Central stopping train in 1937, standing at the platform at Cromford hauled by 2P 4-4-0 No 323. This is an interesting engine as she was built for the Somerset & Dorset Joint Railway in 1906 and is fitted with an exhaust smoke injector. The five engines in this class were rebuilt by Fowler in 1921 and taken into LMS stock in 1930. The four bolts on the tender side are a reminder of SDJR days, and formed the base for the tablet-catcher apparatus used for working over the single lines of that company.

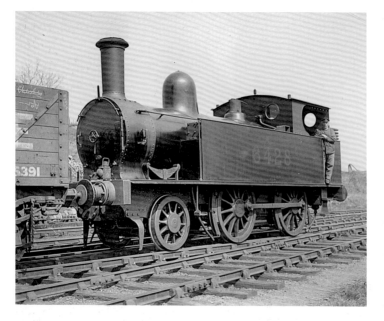

Left Much has been written about the famous Cromford & High Peak Railway, the southern section of which left the Midland main line at High Peak Junction near Cromford; by means of inclines, it traversed the limestone hills of Derbyshire to join the LNWR Ashbourne to Buxton line at Parsley Hay. Standing near Steeplehouse on the C&HPR on 13 April 1933 is ex-LNWR 2-4-0T No 6428, which worked on the line from the mid-1890s until she was withdrawn from service in March 1952. There were 50 engines in this class built by Webb, and subsequently all but ten were rebuilt as 2-4-2 tanks. Of interest is the fact that the section of line over which this engine spent much of its life was short: from the top of the Cromford incline to the bottom of the Middleton incline is a distance of just 1 mile.

Above In the heart of the limestone country, ex-Midland Railway 3F 0-6-0 No 3274 drops down from Millers Dale Junction towards Buxton Junction with a Rowsley to Buxton freight in 1932. Of Johnson design, this particular locomotive was built by Neilson in 1890 and was allocated to Buxton at the time of the photograph. In the background is the River Wye Viaduct carrying the Midland main line to Manchester.

Below Showing a good head of steam, ex-Midland Railway 3F 0-6-0 No 3538 is being banked as it works a freight from Rowsley to the Manchester area through the southernmost end of Great Rocks Dale. Immediately behind this down train is the very short Peak Forest Junction Tunnel, hewn through natural rock, and beyond that Peak Forest Junction signal box, where the line to Buxton leaves the main line. The superb Midland splitting gantry supports Peak Forest Junction's home signals with the distant signals for Millers Dale Junction (off) and Buxton Junction. The siding on the left was used temporarily for dumping spoil from the local quarries. No 3538 was built by Neilson in 1896 and allocated to Shed 20 Buxton when the photograph was taken.

LMS Compound No 1059 heads a St Pancras to Manchester Central express towards Peak Forest in the late 1920s. Eight vehicles was a good load for a Compound, and the engine is being worked hard on the 1 in 90 climb. The area to the right of the train is now occupied by the loading hoppers and sidings belonging to the Tunstead Quarry, which are seen in the second photograph taken in 2001, and which ensure the retention of the railway north from Tunstead. The modern photograph is looking down on the loading facilities and sidings, and shows the precise location of the earlier one taken 70 years previously.

'It's nice to see the light of day' as a down Rowsley to Gowhole freight storms out of Great Rocks Tunnel in 1930; the tunnel, 161 yards in length, is on the Midland main line between Millers Dale and Peak Forest and half way up the long 1 in 90 ascent to the latter location. The two engines are Kirtley 2-4-0 No 84 piloting an LMS 4F 0-6-0. The Kirtley 2-4-0s were built for express passenger work, but No 84, built at Derby in 1866, finished her days at Rowsley assisting down freights over the steeply graded main line through the splendid Derbyshire hills.

Above Two LMS 4F 0-6-0s are hard at work up the 1 in 90 from Chapel-en-le-Frith to Dove Holes Tunnel on the main line in 1938. No 4431, the leading engine, was built at Derby in 1927 and allocated to 16D Mansfield when the photograph was taken. In the distance are two signals: the left-hand one is Chapel-en-le-Frith down distant and the other Dove Holes Tunnel up distant. Shortly the train will pass under the LNWR Manchester to Buxton line, then enter the long Dove Holes Tunnel to emerge at 985 feet above sea level near Peak Forest.

Below The LNWR line from Manchester to Buxton climbs steeply over the long stretch between Whaley Bridge and Dove Holes. Here Fowler 2-6-4T No 2323 approaches Chapel-en-le-Frith (South) with a Buxton-bound express in 1930. No 2323 was built at Derby in 1928; later engines in the class had side-window cabs. The train comprises six LNWR non-corridors, and the LNWR distant signal is that for Chapel (South).

These three pictures are of engines that worked on the construction of the Goyt Valley Reservoir, north-west of Buxton, in the 1930s. Lehane, Mackenzie & Shand was the firm responsible for the work, and the photographs also show the wagons used to move the materials and spoil during the operations. They were all taken at Fernilee in September 1934 on the 3-foot-guage railway.

The first shows *Darley Dale*, an 0-4-0 well tank built by Ducross & Braun in 1925. The second is a portrait of *Kinder*, an 0-4-0 tank built by Orenstein & Koppel of Berlin in 1925 to works number 10903, and the third shows *Vyrnwy*, built by the same maker, also in 1925.

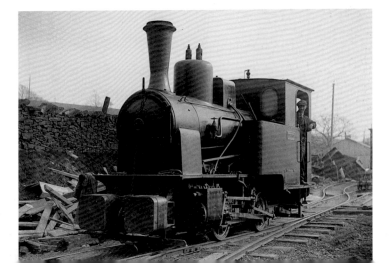

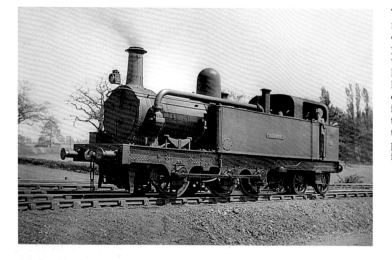

This remarkable engine graced the railways of the Shipley Colliery complex near Ilkeston for many years. An 0-6-4 tank, *Cecil Raikes* was originally built by Beyer Peacock in 1886 for the Mersey Railway. She was fitted with condensing apparatus for working in the tunnels of that railway and the condensing pipes remained on the engine when she was photographed at Shipley Colliery in May 1933.

The ironworks at Stanton near Ilkeston on the Derbyshire/Nottinghamshire border had a large internal railway network and used 27 locomotives, including a crane engine, to work the system. No 22 is a handsome machine; built by Dick Kerr of Stoke-on-Trent, she was photographed at Stanton in May 1935. The copper-capped chimney is of interest, as are the background array of telegraph poles and the usual piles of commercial debris often associated with such busy places.

No 2757 was built by Kirtley for the Midland Railway in 1870. During the First World War 80 of the class were loaned to the government and many saw service overseas. At the end of the war all were repatriated and saw further service into LMS days. However, in the 1920s many were withdrawn and by the time No 2757 was photographed at Shipley Gate on 8 August 1933 she had been awaiting her fate for some while; the word 'Condemned' stencilled on the firebox testifies to this.

3. North Western lines

LMS streamlined 'Pacific' No 6220 *Coronation* was but a few weeks into regular service when the picture was taken in 1937. She has a full head of steam and waits to depart from Euston with an Anglo-Scottish express, host to a crowd of admiring passengers, and the author! The crown above the nameplate identifies this particular member of the class, and later in the year she attained 114mph south of Crewe when on a special test run.

Above A diversion into the complex and busy Staffordshire coalfield. First to Chasetown engine shed for the Cannock Chase Colliery, and home to a most interesting locomotive. Complete with home-made tender, long-boiler No 6, built by Sharp Stewart in 1876, works number 2643, pauses long enough between colliery duties for the photograph to be taken on 6 May 1933. Interestingly, No 6 was not the oldest engine at Cannock Chase – that prize goes to 0-4-2 tank *McClean* built by Beyer Peacock in 1856 and still going strong in 1933.

Below Another extremely old engine working in Staffordshire in June 1935 is 0-4-2 tank *Blackcock*, built by Beyer Peacock in 1871, works number 1140. The photograph was taken at Hednesford & Brindley Heath on the West Cannock Colliery system.

In 1935 there were nine engines based at Rawnsley for work on the Cannock & Rugeley Colliery complex, and two are seen here. *Birch* (*above*) was a 2-4-0 outside-cylinder tank built at the colliery itself in 1888, while *Cannock Wood* was an inside-cylinder 0-6-0 tank. The latter started life on the London, Brighton & South Coast Railway in 1877 and was named *Burgundy*. She was purchased by the Cannock & Rugeley Colliery in 1927, modified and renamed.

Also of interest are the colliery-owned wagons. Up to the time when the whole wagon fleet was 'pooled', each colliery owned its own wagons, which, when empty, had to be shunted out and returned home after each trip.

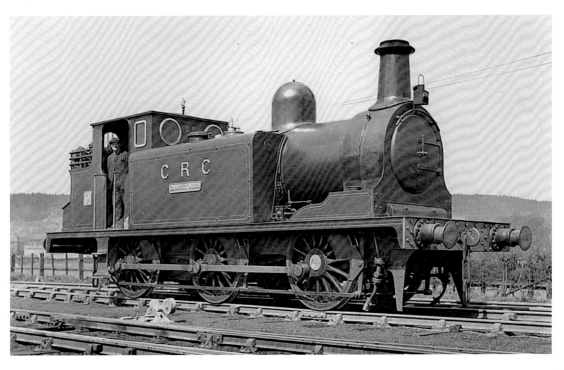

It was just an hour from home in the train for Dad and other railway photographers to get to Tamworth, where two main lines crossed. Having obtained many Midland pictures, particularly north of Derby, Dad concentrated on the former LNWR line and spent many happy hours in the vicinity of Coton Crossing, towards Stafford. The following seven photographs were taken around 1931 and portray a variety of engines and trains at that location.

In the first, small-boilered 'Claughton' No 5903 *Duke of Sutherland*, on an up express, passes one in the opposite direction on the north side of Tamworth.

No 5903 was one of the first of the 130 four-cylinder 'Claughtons' built by Bowen-Cooke between 1913 and 1921; she was then numbered 21 by the LNWR. All received the LMS numbers 5600 to 6029 with the grouping in 1923. These engines did some fine work over many sections of the LMS, and particularly over the ex-LNWR main line for which they were originally built. From 1927, the emergence from the works of the 'Royal Scots' heralded the beginning of the end, and the first to be withdrawn was No 5977 in 1929. Note the signal-wire compensator in the cess.

At the same location an up express is being worked by an unidentified LNWR 'Prince of Wales' Class 4-6-0, piloting a recently built 'Royal Scot'. In 1923 there were 245 'Prince of Wales' locomotives running on the LNWR system; a superheated version of the earlier 'Experiment' 4-6-0s, the first engine, built at Crewe in October 1911, was No 819 *Prince of Wales*.

Above As passenger trains became heavier over the ex-LNWR main line, before the full introduction of the 'Royal Scots' and well prior to the Stanier 'Pacifics', double-heading was commonplace. This 1930 photograph was taken between Tamworth and Coton Crossing, and shows a down express hauled by a Rugby-based 'Precedent' 2-4-0, No 5011 *Director*, and an unidentified 'Prince of Wales' 4-6-0.

Undoubtedly the 'Precedents' were Webb's most successful passenger engine and, considering their small size, did valiant work. The class consisted of 90 locomotives built between 1874 and 1882, and later 96 'Newtons' of the Ramsbottom era were rebuilt to conform to the 'Precedent' design. Two of the best known 'Precedents' were No 955 *Charles Dickens*, which amassed a remarkable 2,300,000 miles in its

relatively short life of 20 years, and No 790 *Hardwicke*, which distinguished itself in the race to Scotland in 1895. Eighty of the class survived into LMS days to become Nos 5000 to 5079, but large-scale withdrawals began soon after. The last engine in service was No 5001 *Snowdon*, broken up in 1936.

Below No 5011 is seen again, this time piloting a small-boilered 'Claughton' on a down express just north of Tamworth. Of interest are the destination boards on the carriage roofs and the distant signal, its remarkable height allowing good sighting on the approach to Tamworth. A requirement for the job of lampman or signal maintenance staff was certainly a head for heights!

In the cutting north of Tamworth, No 5011 again acts as pilot engine on a down express.
On this occasion the train engine is one of the LNWR large-boilered 4-6-0 Caprotti 'Claughtons'.

Above The engines built to relieve the chronic motive power situation on the ex-LNWR main line were the 'Royal Scots'. The first 50 came out in 1927, followed by 20 more in 1930. Here No 6122 *Royal Ulster Rifleman* makes light work of a Manchester to Euston express on the approach to Tamworth in 1931. This particular engine was built by the North British Locomotive Company in 1927. It is interesting to see, following many experiments, how the smoke deflectors were successful in taking the exhaust up and away from the driver's line of vision.

Below The exact location is uncertain, but this is a lovely shot of an unrebuilt 'Claughton' working hard on an express in the late 1920s. The engine has been rebuilt with a Belpaire boiler and is unnamed, but retains its LNWR number plate on the cab side.

Above Approaching Basford Hall Junction, Crewe, with an up relief express in 1937 is unrebuilt 'Royal Scot' No 6136 *The Border Regiment*. Many thought the unrebuilt 'Scots' to be exceedingly handsome engines, and this example was built by the North British Locomotive Company in 1927 and originally named *Goliath* after a Webb Compound 'Jubilee'.

Twenty-five of the 'Royal Scots' had names commemorating early LNWR locomotives with brass plaques bearing an etched outline of the engine in question; these were replaced by regimental names in 1935/6. The first 'Royal Scot' to be withdrawn was in 1962, and the final one went in 1965.

Below Following his appointment to CM&EE of the LMS, one of Stanier's first designs was the four-cylinder 'Princess Royal' 4-6-2 'Pacific'. The first two

came out in 1933 and, after extensive trials, ten more were delivered in 1935. Concurrently with this second batch appeared No 6202, which differed radically in that she was propelled by non-condensing steam turbines, a large one on the left of the engine for forward running and a smaller on the right for reverse.

However, problems resulted in her being in the works for lengthy periods, but when she was in service she was considered to be an extremely capable machine. She ran as a turbine engine until 1952, and was then rebuilt with the normal four cylinders and motion. She became *Princess Anne*, and as such was tragically destroyed in the Harrow & Wealdstone accident later that year. She is seen here at Basford Hall Junction in 1936 working a Liverpool to Euston express.

Above Albeit home to engines mainly for freight work, Crewe South was an extremely busy and important locomotive depot. Somewhat overshadowed by its sister passenger shed at the other end of the station, nevertheless the South shed could provide an astonishing variety of motive power from a whole range of other depots on the LMS system.

Here in 1932 is 0-6-0 No 4211, from a Midland Railway design, built by Fowler at Derby in 1925, ready to work 442 Special, perhaps to a holiday resort. The Derby 4Fs were quite capable of hauling special passenger trains and regularly did so at holiday times to Blackpool and along the North Wales coast.

Behind No 4211 is an LMS 0-8-0 freight locomotive commonly known as an 'Austin 7'. They were numbered in the 95xx series and the class totalled 175 engines. Introduced for working heavy coal traffic over the former Lancashire & Yorkshire system, the engines were all built at Crewe between 1929 and 1932, and the example in this photograph is almost certainly on a running-in turn following delivery to traffic.

Below A visit to Crewe South shed on 7 April 1934 revealed a stranger in the form of ex-Midland Railway 2F 0-6-0 No 3479. She is already fully coaled and crewed up ready for her next turn of duty.

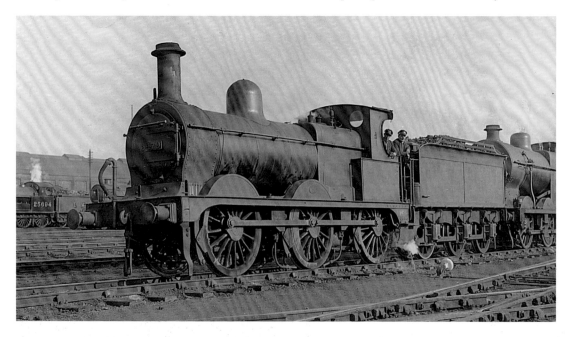

Above On the same date in April 1934, large-boilered 'Claughton' No 6004 *Princess Louise* is waiting her turn to go on to the turntable then the ash-pit prior to her next working. At this time she was a Longsight Shed 16 engine.

Bowen-Cooke's 'Claughtons' were the largest passenger engines built for the LNWR, and 130 were built between 1913 and 1921. In 1928 20 of the class were rebuilt with larger boilers, and No 6004 was one of those, and also the last 'Claughton' to remain in service. She lasted eight years after the previous withdrawal and was finally broken up in 1949.

Below Sister engine No 5910 *J. A. Bright*, a Bangor (Shed 21) engine, is having the coal levelled and brought forward before going on to the ash-pit at Crewe South in April 1934. She was built in August 1914, went into traffic as LNWR No 250, was reboilered in 1928, and was a Carlisle Upperby engine for some years. Both are unmodified to the extent that they retained the Walschaerts valve gear when they were reboilered, and were not given Caprotti valve gear.

Above Being prepared for work on Crewe South shed in April 1934 is Stanier 2-6-0 No 13245. This was Stanier's first design for the LMS, having previously been on the Great Western at Swindon. No 13245 (later 2945) was one of a class of 40 engines built at Crewe in 1932/34, and the first ten had the safety valves and top feed to the dome combined.

Below The pleasing lines of the 'Baby Scots' are display in this photograph of No 5545 at Crewe 1936. Painted red and based at 9A Longsight, s awaits the signal to go to the station to work t W912(1) Special. She was later rebuilt with a larg taper boiler and received the name *Planet*.

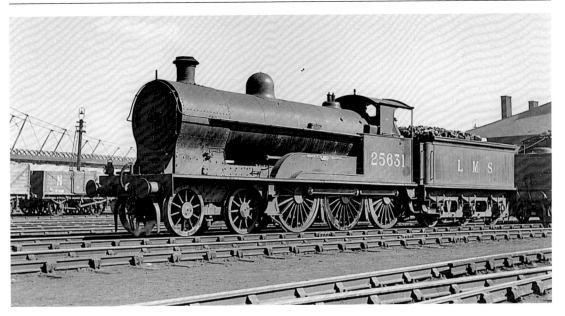

Above At the other end of Crewe station was North shed, the elite 5A depot, where locomotives for express passenger working over the whole of the West Coast Main Line prevailed. The location is identified by the overbridge that ran from the station platforms into the locomotive works; an 18-inch narrow-gauge railway ran on the unusual suspension bridge conveying stores and locomotive parts to and from the works.

Former LNWR 'Prince of Wales' 4-6-0 No 25631 *Felicia Hermans*, retaining the round-topped boiler, sits on North shed in 1934, crewed up to work her next turn of duty. The 'Prince of Wales' engines followed the 'Experiments' and had large piston valves, bigger cylinders, extended smokebox and superheater, and this example was built by Bowen-Cooke in 1914 as LNWR No 1400.

Below On the same day in 1934, Fowler 2P 4-4-0 No 653 shows off her graceful lines and her origins from a successful Midland Railway design. This engine was built at Crewe in 1931, and the whole class consisted of 138 engines, three of which were built for the Somerset & Dorset Joint Railway. Two members of the class, Nos 633 and 653, were fitted with the Dabeg feedwater-heater equipment, which can clearly be seen on the smokebox side. Two others, Nos 591 and 639, were involved in a collision in 1934 and were so badly damaged that they were withdrawn from service. The remainder all survived into BR days and withdrawal did not occur on any scale until 1958.

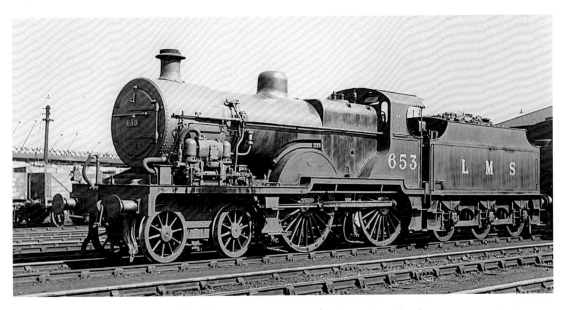

Above These two locomotives make a fine sight as they wait to drop back into Crewe station to work an express to the north on 7 April 1934. The engines are LMS 4-4-0 No 654, with 6ft 9in driving wheels, coupled to an ex-LNWR 'Prince of Wales' 4-6-0. No 654's '15' shedplate clearly indicates that the 4-4-0 is allocated to Crewe North.

Below With the iron foundry building behind, the scene is the yard in Crewe Locomotive Works on 2 August 1933, where a pair of smaller-boilered 'Claughtons' await repair or – more likely withdrawal. In a little over 12 months from the date of this photograph, all the small-boilered members of the class had been taken out of service, and only the 2 large-boilered engines remained. The two seen here are Nos 5919 *Lord Kitchener*, built in 1914 as LNWR No 2401, and unnamed 5984, built in 1919.

Amongst the chimneys, buildings and materials associated with locomotive works yards, 0-4-0 shunting tank No 3084, with associated tender, stands alongside her personal supply of steam coal.

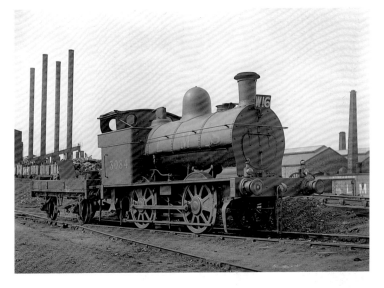

A class of locomotive built specifically for short-haul freight work in Lancashire and in both North and South Wales was the Webb 0-6-2 'Coal Tank'. An 1881 design, 300 were built in the years to 1896, and they were remarkable for the fact that, apart from two fitted with widened side tanks, the whole class remained unaltered throughout its whole career. All but one were withdrawn by 1955. No 7803, later 58926, was photographed at Llandudno Junction on 12 June 1935, and lasted for four further years.

The passenger equivalent of the coal tanks was a class of 0-6-2 tank locomotives with 5ft 2in driving wheels built at Crewe between 1898 and 1902. These were good engines and were originally designed for the intensive Euston to Watford and Birmingham to Sutton Coldfield suburban services; it is on record that when working those services they were required to stop and start nearly 100 times in a little over 200 miles. Many passed into BR hands in 1948 and the final withdrawal came in 1953.

The driver and fireman appear relaxed with their more than adequately coaled mount and are quite happy to pose before proceeding with their next local passenger turn.

Above This late-1920s photograph shows the down 'Lakes Express' on Dillicar water troughs between Low Gill and Tebay. The engine is a general utility 4-6-2 tank built by Bowen-Cooke for the LNWR, No 6959. These engines were unusual in that they were fitted with variable blastpipes; by raising or lowering a central cone in the blastpipe, the driver could sharpen or soften the blast according to running conditions. In addition they were fitted with a Duplex water pick-up scoop, which worked whether the engine was running chimney-first or bunker-first.

Below The Lancashire & Yorkshire Railway 4-6-0 four-cylinder passenger engines were known as the 'Dreadnoughts'. Originally built for the L&Y main line, they later provided sterling service over the

LNWR main line over Shap. Twenty were built at Horwich in 1908/09 as L&Y Nos 1506-25. In 1922 No 1506 was superheated, and 35 more appeared in 1923/24 at the time of the grouping, then a further 20 in 1924/25.

Under the LMS numbering scheme they become Nos 10400 to 10474. The first five (Nos 10400-10404) were withdrawn as early as 1925, and all the others had gone by 1939 with the exception of No 10455, which remained in service until 1951. The engine in the photograph, taken at Carlisle Upperby on 16 July 1933, is No 10456. Built at Horwich in August 1924 and two years later rebuilt as a four-cylinder compound, she performed admirably over the LNWR main line north of Crewe until her withdrawal from service in March 1936.

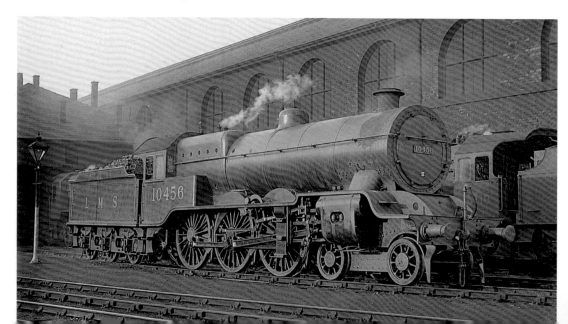

4. Welsh lines

Dad loved to visit North Wales, which, as he so aptly put it, was the home of the friendly and tenacious railways. It must have been exceptionally hard to work in the Snowdonia slate quarries as the weather was frequently inclement, yet he delighted in talking to the men there, riding on their engines and photographing the scene. He spent many wonderful days 'away from all that main-line stuff'.

A visit to the Snowdon Mountain Railway on 12 June 1935 found Nos 6 *Padarn* and 7 *Aylwin* in the station at Llanberis. Both engines were built at Winterthur in Switzerland in 1922/23 especially for this famous North Wales mountain railway, and both were superheated and fitted with shorter side tanks. Worked on the Abt rack system, the Snowdon Mountain Railway was opened in 1895 and built to a gauge of 2ft 7½in.

Above and above right Very close to Llanberis, the Dinorwic quarries boasted a fascinating railway system. At various altitudes high on adjacent mountainsides puffs of smoke could be seen as the quarry engines went about their business. These galleries were served by a 1ft 10⅜in-gauge railway, and the slates were loaded on to wagons and hauled down the hill, eventually to Gilfach Ddu marshalling yard. There the wagons were loaded on to 4ft 0in-gauge vehicles and worked over the 6-mile Padarn Railway to the sea at Port Dinorwic.

Two of the 20 locomotives that worked in the slate galleries were photographed on 14 July 1933. *Covertcoat* (*above*) was Hunslet-built in 1898, works number 679. Originally she was named *The Second*, and was eventually sold for preservation in 1964. *Wild*

Aster (*above right*) was also a Hunslet engine, dating from 1904, works number 849. She was unfit for further service in 1961 and was sold for preservation in 1969.

Right Having arrived from the quarries, the 1ft 10⅜in vehicles were loaded on to the 4ft 0in wagons at Gilfach Ddu, Llanberis, for onward working to Port Dinorwic along the Padarn Railway. 4ft 0in-gauge engines worked this line in 1935, and one of them, *Velinheli*, was photographed at Gilfach Ddu on 12 June of that year. She was built at Hunslet in 1895, works number 631, and worked on the line until she was dismantled for repair in 1953. The engine was never re-assembled and was finally broken up in 1963. The small loaded quarry wagons can be seen on the 'main-line' wagons in the background.

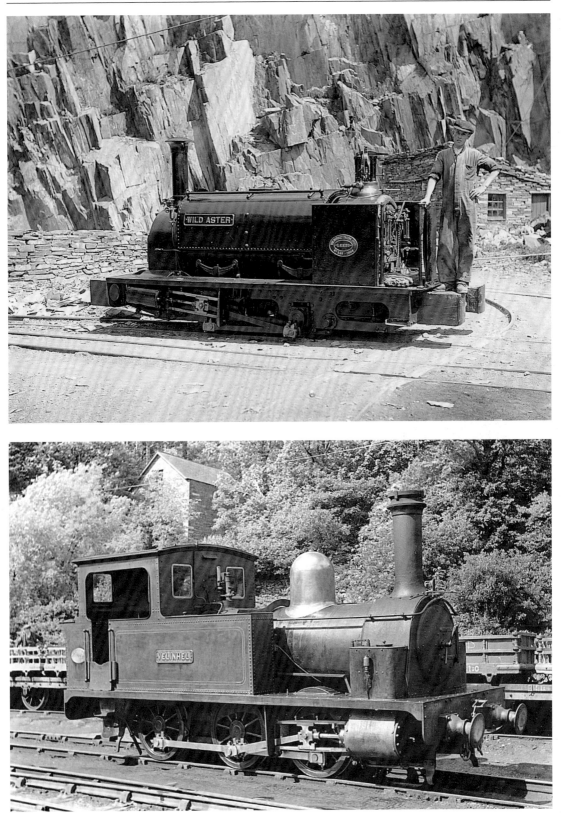

Above Another slate quarry with an extensive railway system was the Penrhyn at Bethesda. In this case the whole network was of 1ft 10¾in gauge and the wagons, once loaded in the quarry, were eventually moved along the Penrhyn Railway to the sea at Port Penrhyn.

In 1934 some 28 locomotives were engaged on this extensive railway, and here we see *Margaret*, built by Hunslet in 1894, works number 605. As with many quarry engines, the driver had absolutely no protection from the elements, and the weather in that area could frequently be bad!

Below Eigiau was built by Orenstein & Koppel of Berlin in 1912, works number 5668. She was the only Orenstein & Koppel-built engine ever to work in North Wales, and was acquired from the Aluminium Works at Llyn Cowlyd Twy in 1929. She was taken out of service and dumped in 1960, but was subsequently preserved and is now at Bressingham Steam Museum.

Above Seen derelict and in rather a sorry state at Bethesda on 10 July 1934 is 2-6-2 tank *Tregarth*. Built by Baldwin's of Philadelphia, USA, in 1917, works number 46764, she was acquired by the Penrhyn Quarry Company in 1923 and worked the Penrhyn line from Bethesda to Port Penrhyn until withdrawal in 1928 and finally scrapped in 1940.

Below *Linda* also worked the 5-mile line from Bethesda to Port Penrhyn. Hunslet-built in 1893, works number 590, she was withdrawn in 1962 and is now with the Ffestiniog Railway.

Two remarkable engines that worked on the Pen-yr-Orsedd quarry's 2ft 0in-gauge system at Nantlle were 0-4-0 vertical-boiler well tanks, of which the quarry owned five. *Inverlochy* was built by De Winton of Caernarvon in 1877 and sister engine *Gelli* by the same firm in 1893. They were photographed at Nantlle on 12 June 1935.

Constructed by the lesser-known firm of G. B. Longridge & Co, *Prince Albert* was a 7ft 0in broad gauge 0-4-0 well tank. She was built specifically for the construction of the breakwater at Holyhead and was owned by the Holyhead Silica Company. It is thought that the broad gauge line was discontinued in 1912, so the locomotive had been out of service for many years when the first photograph was taken, and for nearly 24 when the second was taken in June 1935. By then she really had succumbed to the vandals and to the elements.

Above The Shropshire & Montgomeryshire Light Railway had a somewhat chequered start. Built originally as the Potteries, Salop & North Wales Railway, this standard gauge line was opened from Shrewsbury to Blodwell in 1866, only to be closed in 1880. It then re-opened in 1911 as the Shropshire & Montgomeryshire from Shrewsbury to Llanymynech. It closed to passengers in 1934, although occasional trains did run thereafter. Final closure of the line and the Criggion branch took place in 1960.

One of the locomotives to run on the S&M was Ilfracombe Goods 0-6-0 No 4 *Thisbe*. Built for the London & South Western Railway by Beyer Peacock in 1875, she came to the Shropshire & Montgomeryshire when the line opened in 1911 and remained until closure. She was photographed at Kinnerley on 18 April 1935.

Below The Bishops Castle Railway was also of standard gauge, and ran from Craven Arms to Bishops Castle in Central Wales. The line was opened on 1 February 1866 and *Carlisle* was purchased for the railway in 1895; she was built as an 0-6-0 saddle tank in 1868 by Kitson, but was later rebuilt as a tender engine. She was painted dark green and interestingly, when repairs were needed, she had to go to the workshops of the Wrexham, Mold & Connah's Quay Railway in Wrexham. However, it is said that the BCR engines later went to Stafford Rd, Wolverhampton, for repairs, hence the chimney, dome and lubricator, and GWR vacuum brake system. Next to the engine is an ex-LSWR passenger six-wheeler. *Carlisle* survived until the line was closed in 1936 when she was broken up.

5. LNER miscellany

To photograph trains on the LNER main line, Dad invariably went to Grantham. It was a straightforward train ride over the old GN line from Derby Friargate, but, once there, he would abandon the station environment for the preferred rural setting of the southbound climb to Stoke Tunnel and the pleasant surroundings of the Peascliffe Tunnel/Barkston area to the north. Many expresses changed engines in both directions at Grantham, and the scene of a fairly cold engine, fresh off the shed

and working hard, particularly on the climb to Stoke, enabled him to capture some graphic steam and smoke effects.

Here is a fine shot of a Gresley 'A1' 'Pacific' climbing Stoke with an up express in about 1933 behind No 2555 *Centenary*, built at Doncaster in 1925. Under the LNER renumbering of 1946/47 *Centenary* became 56, and later 60056. Next to the locomotive is an ex-GNR full Brake six-wheeler followed by a Post Office vehicle.

This truly fine shot portrays Gresley 'A1' 'Pacific' No 2548 *Galtee More* climbing Stoke bank prior to 1928 with a Newcastle to King's Cross express. The 'A1s' were the final design for the Great Northern Railway when two engines with 180lb boiler pressure were built in 1922. Ten more followed in 1923, and 40 more in the next two years.

Following trials on the Great Western, in 1927 No 4480 was rebuilt with a 220lb boiler and this heralded the building of the 'A3' 'super Pacific'. In consequence, all engines built after 1928 were 'A3s', and all the earlier 'A1s' were eventually reboilered. No 2548 was built in 1924 and the photograph shows her with the original 180lb boiler. The vehicle next to the engine is an ex-GNR clerestory bogie Brake.

Taken near Saltersford just south of Grantham in 1931, this photograph depicts Gresley 'K3' 2-6-0 No 167 climbing steadily up the bank with a King's Cross-bound express, composed mainly of GNR six-wheelers. The 'K3' was a powerful mixed-traffic engine and, when built, had the largest boiler yet seen in this country. In addition, it was the first class to feature Gresley's famous 2-to-1 conjugated valve gear: the piston valves of the inside cylinders were activated by levers connected to the tail rods of the outside-cylinder valve gear, which dispensed with the need for separate valve gear for the inside cylinders, and the design was fitted to most Gresley three-cylinder locomotives.

Ten 'K3s' were built for the GNR in 1920, and after the grouping a further 183 were built for the LNER up to 1937. No 167 was built at Darlington in March 1925, became No 1850 in 1946 and was withdrawn in June 1961. The locomotive retains her pre-1928 livery with the number on the tender.

Of great interest in the photograph are the GNR 'somersault' signals for Saltersford on the up and Grantham South on the down. While the top arms were at a great height for sighting purposes, it was the practice for the spectacle glasses and lamps to be mounted further down the post.

Above The up Leeds-King's Cross 'Yorkshire Pullman' presents a heavy load for green ex-GNR 'C1' 'Atlantic' No 4450 photographed near Great Ponton on the climb to Stoke Tunnel.

It was in 1902 that the first of the larger and better-known Ivatt 'Atlantics' were built. They were the largest passenger engine in service in the country at the time and did yeoman work over the GN main line for many years. An essential feature of the class was the wide firebox, which enabled provision of a larger grate and the bigger boiler; these contributed much to the success of the design, which eventually totalled 94 engines. Withdrawal began in 1945, but 17 survived into BR stock in 1948. However, this situation didn't last long and the final locomotive was withdrawn from service in 1950.

Below Another Ivatt 'C1' 'Atlantic', No 4456, strides up Stoke bank with a Doncaster to Peterborough stopping train. Numerically the 'C1s' were the largest class of passenger engine inherited by the LNER at the grouping in 1923. The train is comprised of a veritable assortment of ex-GNR rolling-stock, including six-wheelers and clerestory vehicles.

Above North of Grantham the gradients are more favourable and an essential rural background sets the scene for the passage of a Gresley 'A1' 'Pacific' on a King's Cross to Newcastle express in 1932. The engine is No 2543 *Melton*, the first of a batch of 40 'Pacifics' built in 1924/25. Former GN clerestory bogie vehicles are included in the train formation.

Below Having left Peascliffe Tunnel, a down local stopping train is trundled northwards behind Ivatt 'D2' 4-4-0 No 4323 with a rake of GN stock, including Brakes. In all, Ivatt built 177 4-4-0s for the GNR between 1896 and 1911, of which 70 were of Class 'D2'. This particular engine became No 2153 under the LNER renumbering, but was withdrawn in the early 1950s.

With the ex-GNR Barkston South Junction somersault distant signal in the background, and hauling a rake of Gresley LNER stock, the up 'Flying Scotsman' steps out towards Grantham in the late 1930s hauled by Gresley 'A3' 'Pacific' No 2796 *Spearmint*. She was a Haymarket engine and would have worked through from Edinburgh with this service.

Above An up local passenger train with a very odd collection of rolling-stock nears Peascliffe Tunnel hauled by Ivatt 4-4-2 'Atlantic' No 3271, which itself was an odd locomotive. The first tender engine of the 4-4-2 wheel arrangement to run in Britain was Ivatt's No 990, which emerged from Doncaster in 1898. The type had already established a firm footing in America, and thus more of the '990' Class appeared after the turn of the century. However, in 1902 a more powerful engine appeared in the form of No 271 (later 3271). She was similar in appearance to the other members of the '990' Class, but had four high-pressure cylinders and Walschaerts valve gear. This engine remained the only one of the class so fitted, but after various modifications was ultimately rebuilt with two inside cylinders in 1911, as seen in this photograph. She was finally broken up in 1936.

Right Another interesting Ivatt large-boilered 'Atlantic' was No 279, built at Doncaster in 1905. Ivatt experimented with other members of the class, and in 1915 rebuilt No 279 (later 3279) as a four-cylinder simple machine fitted with a 24-element Robinson superheater. In addition, the two sets of Walschaerts valve gear on the inside were driven from the outside Walschaerts motion. She reverted to two cylinders in 1937 and was finally withdrawn from service in 1948, having been a New England (Peterborough) engine for many years. She is seen here at Peterborough on 16 June 1935 surrounded by a host of ex-GNR somersault signals, including a superb gantry.

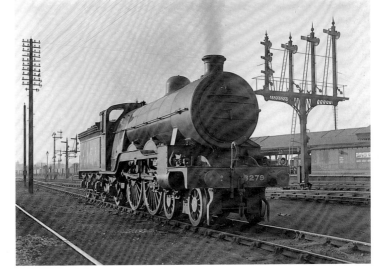

Above Looking to provide a high-speed service between King's Cross and Newcastle, Gresley produced his first famous streamlined 'Pacifics' in 1935. There were four in the original batch, followed by others in 1937 to establish a non-stop service from the capital to Edinburgh. Eventually a total of 35 were built, and all lasted well into BR days except No 4469, which was destroyed in an air raid on York in 1942.

Literally only a few days after delivery into traffic, an SLS visit to King's Cross shed on 14 September 1935 found No 2509 *Silver Link* being prepared for work. Just two weeks later this engine attained a maximum of 112½mph and sustained an average of 100mph for 43 miles while on a test run.

Below Many enthusiasts regard the Robinson engines of the Great Central Railway as being among some of the most handsome. Not so, this beast! Robinson built six 'B3' 4-6-0 'Lord Faringdon' Class engines for the Great Central main line in 1917, with four cylinders and 6ft 9in driving wheels. In 1929 two – Nos 6166 and 6167 – were rebuilt with Caprotti valve gear, which apparently brought a distinct improvement in the performance of a class of engine that had something of a shabby reputation. One of the Caprotti engines, No 6167, is photographed at Leicester (GC) shed in 1933.

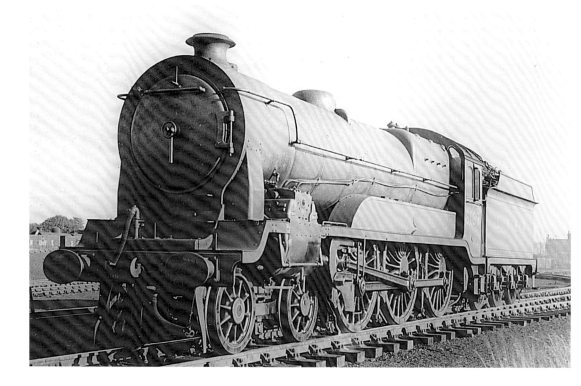

Above The 'B4' 4-6-0s of the Great Central Railway were fine-looking locomotives. Built by Robinson in 1906 they were two-cylinder machines with 6ft 7in driving wheels. There were ten in the class, which became known as the 'Imminghams', and fine work is recorded over the GC main line. No 6097 was in fact named *Immingham*, and here we see No 6099, a Copley Hill engine, working a day excursion to King's Cross from Leeds, near Peascliffe.

Below The graceful lines of an 'Immingham' 'B4' 4-6-0 in LNER green livery are highlighted in this photograph of No 6104.

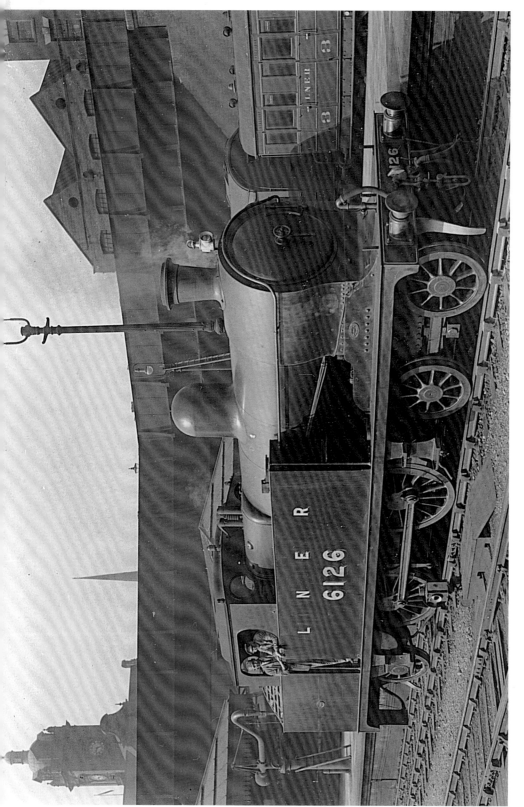

The vast Nottingham Victoria station was often busy and always full of interest, lying as it did between the tunnels where the Great Central main line was crossed by the Great Northern from Derby to Grantham and where engines from both companies ruled the day. Driver Wilce and his mate pose with smart-looking GCR 4-4-2 tank No 6126. These engines were built by Robinson in 1907 and eventually there were 12 in the class. They all survived into nationalisation, the last being withdrawn in 1960. The imposing station buildings and renowned clock-tower were memorials to an age of remarkable railway architecture; the clock tower still survives above today's Victoria Shopping Centre.

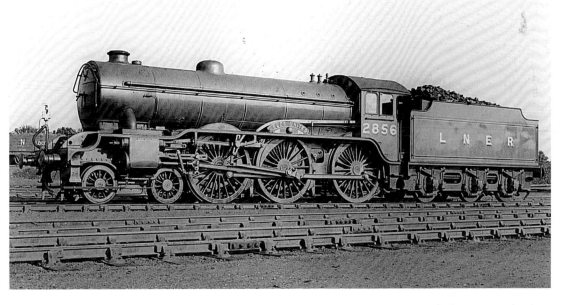

Above For some time after the grouping there had been a growing need for a more powerful locomotive for the Great Eastern section of the LNER. There were, however, severe difficulties imposed by the civil engineer in regard to axle-loadings and engine lengths over this railway. This was largely overcome by Gresley building a class of 4-6-0 passenger engines that were better balanced and reduced the 'hammer-blow' effect on the track. This was achieved to some extent by dividing the drive, whereby the outside cylinders and motion drove the centre driving wheels and the inside ones the leading pair.

There followed another 47, which were all allocated to the GER and were named after places and buildings with an East Anglian connection. Then, in 1936, 25 additional 'B17s' were built at Darlington and fitted with a larger 4,200-gallon tender; these engines were mostly named after English football clubs. No 2856 *Leeds United*, lined out and in LNER apple green, was photographed at Leicester (GC) shed not long after initial delivery.

Below Sister engine No 2848 *Arsenal* looks particularly smart with her 4,200-gallon tender at Doncaster in 1938.

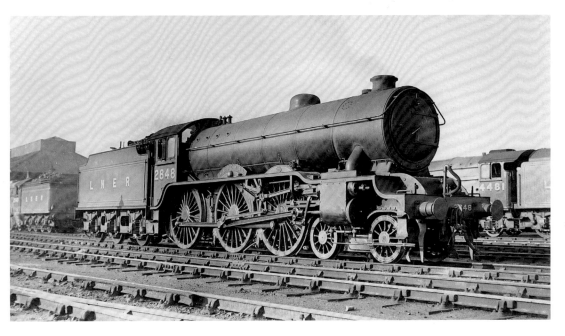

Above The 'W1' 4-6-4 four-cylinder high-pressure locomotive seen earlier at the Wavertree exhibition in 1930 (see page 71) was rebuilt as a conventional three-cylinder engine with a 250lb boiler pressure at Doncaster in 1937, and altered substantially. Her driver and mate look more than pleased to be photographed as they prepare to leave Doncaster shed prior to working an express to King's Cross.

Below 'Right to the top, mate!' Ivatt small-boilered '990' Class 'Atlantic' No 3258 takes water at Doncaster in the mid-1930s. Built at Doncaster in 1903 as No 258, she became 3258 at the grouping and was withdrawn in April 1937.

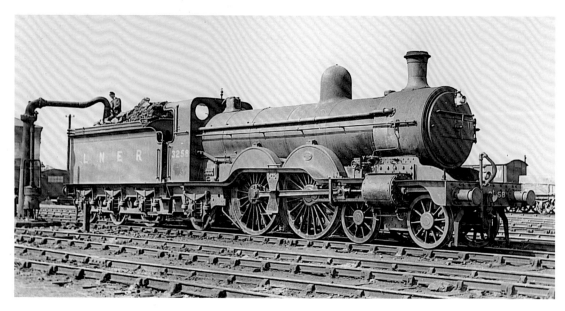

Two former Great Central Railway engines grace the north end of Doncaster shed in 1937. In the background is a Robinson 'O4' 2-8-0 freight locomotive, but centre stage goes to a 'D10' 4-4-0 of the 'Director' Class, a reference to the fact that some of the class were named after directors of the company. The first ten, built by Robinson at Gorton, came out in 1913 as Nos 429 to 438. They were superheated from the outset. They then became Nos 5429 to 5438, and the photograph is of No 5432 *Sir Edward Fraser*.

A slightly larger version appeared between 1919 and 1922, consisting of 11 engines that became 'D11' 4-4-0s. After the grouping of 1923 a further batch of 24 were built for work over the former North British lines in Scotland; it was necessary for these engines to have their boiler mountings reduced in height to suit the more restrictive loading gauge. All the original ten had been withdrawn by 1955.

Above The 'C12' 4-4-2Ts were Ivatt's first design of
tank engine for working the Great Northern Railway's
London suburban services and also some of the more
steeply graded lines in West Yorkshire. In all 60 were
built between 1898 and 1907, and some were
originally fitted with condensing apparatus and
shorter chimneys for working over the 'Widened
Lines' in London. Later the condensing gear was
removed. A rather smart and recently repainted
member of the class, No 4538, acts as shed shunt at
Doncaster in 1935. All the class had gone by 1958.

Below Here is an unusual locomotive on such a
prestigious working: the author stands on the buffer-
beam of Horwich 2-6-0 No 2727 at Sheffield Victoria on
5 May 1948, the engine having worked 'The South
Yorkshireman' over the Great Central main line from
Leicester. The shedplate, 25F, indicates that she
belonged to Low Moor (Bradford) at the time.

Above Opened in 1895, the Hull & Barnsley Railway was built primarily to serve part of the extremely busy South Yorkshire coalfield. Interestingly, only one locomotive engineer, Matthew Stirling, held that post in the company, serving the full 37 years until the company's absorption into the NER in 1922, shortly before the grouping that found them both part of the LNER.

Standing on Doncaster shed in the mid-1930s is one of Stirling's 'L' Class 0-6-0s, No 2418, which retains its original domeless boiler. She was scrapped in 1938.

Below No 2422 of the same class has been rebuilt with a domed boiler, new chimney and altered cab spectacle glasses. She was scrapped in 1937.

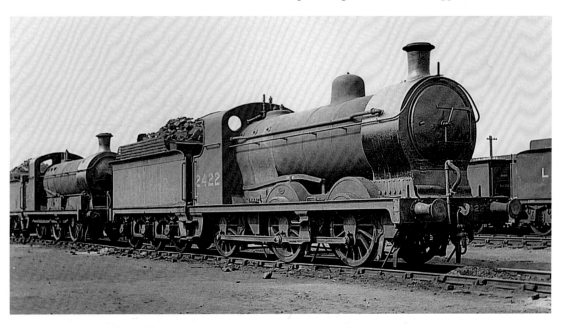

Above Very few locomotives rejoiced in their identification as No 0! However, the famous No 0 at Rothervale Colliery did so, and was photographed at Treeton in 1936. She was built by Beyer Peacock in 1879, works number 1830, and rebuilt by the Yorkshire Engine Company in 1910. She worked at the colliery until the 1950s. Together with engines from two collieries in North Nottinghamshire, those in the West Riding were taken over by the NCB in 1947 and became part of the NE Division.

Below This quite remarkable inside-cylinder 4-4-0 saddle tank worked at Micklefield Colliery and was photographed there on 4 July 1935. The driver is quite undismayed by his strange-looking steed, and at least he has excellent, if somewhat makeshift, protection from the elements. *Emlyn* was built at Stephenson's in 1870, works number 1959, then rebuilt in 1902 and 1925. She worked at Micklefield until 1 July 1939, then lay derelict through the war and was ultimately scrapped at the end of 1945. Upon the formation of the NCB, Micklefield was one of the pits in the No 8 Castleford area. Note the ex-North Eastern Railway signals on the adjacent Leeds to Hull line in the background.

These two engines worked at the Briggs Colliery at Whitwood, which came into the Castleford area of the NCB in 1947. Both were built for the Mersey Railway in 1892 for hauling passenger trains through the tunnel under the river, and as such were fitted with condensing apparatus. When the Mersey Railway was electrified in 1904 both engines came to Briggs and remained there to the end of their lives. They were photographed at Whitwood on 4 July 1935.

Whitwood (*above*), a 2-6-2T built by Kitson in 1892, works number 3394, had been Mersey Railway No 17 *Burnley*; she was scrapped in May 1952. Sister engine *Dorothy*, also a 2-6-2T built by Kitson in 1892, works number 3395, had been Mersey Railway No 18 *Banstead*, and lasted until April 1947. Even in 1935 the engines retained the condensing pipes across the boiler from one side tank to the other.

6. The North East

Above A study of front ends at York: three very different engines, a Gresley 'V2' 2-6-2 mixed-traffic locomotive, a 'J39' 0-6-0 freight engine, and Worsdell 'D20' 4-4-0 No 2106 stand together on the shed there in 1938.

There were 60 engines in W. Worsdell's 'D20' Class, built for the North Eastern Railway; intended as express passenger engines, 30 came out in 1899 followed by a second 30 in 1906. No 2106 was one of the early batch and came into traffic right on the turn of the century. They were undoubtedly the finest of the NER 4-4-0s, taking their turn on main-line expresses for many years.

Above right Originally NER 'R' Class, the 'D20s' certainly proved their worth and frequently worked expresses from Leeds through to Edinburgh. No 724 is seen passing a superb NE distant signal with a heavy train.

Right Coats really shouldn't be left against roof pillars when taking photographs of small boys and big steam engines at York! The author seems dutifully impressed with both the driver and his charge – in this case No 4462 *Great Snipe*, one of Gresley's 'A4' 'Pacifics', on a King's Cross-Newcastle express in 1938. This engine was later renamed *William Whitelaw* and became No 4 under the LNER renumbering of 1946.

Above The following four photographs show an array of North Eastern Railway engines at Darlington on a visit to the shed there on 22 July 1933. In the first is 'B13' 4-6-0 No 761, of the NER 'S' Class, of which there were 40 examples. All were built at Gateshead, 10 in 1899/1900 and 30 more in 1906/09; No 761 was an engine from the later batch.

The 'S' 4-6-0s were notable for being the first dedicated passenger locomotive of that wheel arrangement in the country – a type that was universal in later years. All were taken out of service prior to 1938 except for No 761, which was retained for use as a dummy counter-pressure engine and was used in locomotive tests at both Darlington and at Rugby before being withdrawn in 1951.

Below Built by Worsdell as an express passenger engine for the NER in 1903, 'C6' 4-4-2 No 1753 had 6ft 10in driving wheels and two cylinders. When photographed in 1933 she was painted in LNER green.

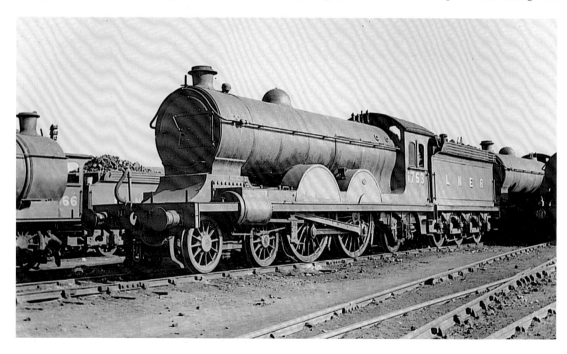

Also in green livery, here is a further example of a Worsdell two-cylinder 'C6' 4-4-2. This engine, photographed at Gateshead in the early 1930s, in No 702.

Above No 2172 is a NER 'Z' Class 4-4-2, of which 53 were built by Raven between 1911 and 1918. With 6ft 10in driving wheels and three cylinders, this class was the prime express passenger power for the NER at the grouping.

Below An interesting wheel arrangement, 4-4-4 tanks were quite uncommon, but 45 were built by Raven for the NER between 1913 and 1921; they were NER Class 'H' and had three cylinders. They were subsequently rebuilt by Gresley as three-cylinder 4-6-2 tanks and became Class 'A8'. The whole class lasted well into BR days and performed more than adequately on local passenger trains in the North East. The engine at Darlington in 1933 is No 1524.

A wagonload of hay next to the chimney of a steam engine doesn't seem to be too good an idea! The Easingwold Railway left the LNER main line at Alne and ran 2½ miles north-eastwards to Easingwold. It was standard gauge and opened in 1891; there was no signalling and the journey time for a passenger train was 8 minutes.

The first engine for the line was a Hudswell Clarke 0-6-0 tank, built in 1891. This was sold in 1903 and replaced by No 2, another Hudswell Clarke engine of 1903, which soldiered on, very much alone, until closure. Photographed at Easingwold on 22 July 1934, No 2 is painted green, but the rolling-stock was red.

Above There was something rather special about the locomotives that worked in the Durham and Northumberland coalfields, so much so that Dad was drawn time and time again to this exciting and varied area. There were places that built their own engines, railways that had their own comprehensive signalling systems, and in some cases engine sheds very much on a par with their larger cousins on the main-line system. It was this variety that appealed most, particularly as some of the engines working the lines had started life with one of the main-line railways and were finishing their life working equally hard for the industrial world.

In the early part of the 19th century the town and port of Seaham was built by the Third Marquess of Londonderry to provide a transport outlet for considerable quantities of coal mined in the extensive coalfields he owned in the County of Durham. Just less than a century later, with the decline in the old collieries and the need for extensive investment in the port at Seaham, the family made sweeping changes and set up the Seaham Harbour Dock Company. Prior to this, the Londonderry locomotive works – an engine shed and well-equipped workshop – was built near Seaham station, and not only undertook major engine repairs but also constructed completely new ones. Dock traffic at Seaham ended in 1992.

In 1933 there were a dozen or so locomotives working in the actual dock area, dealing with traffic from the collieries via the Londonderry Railway and also the South Hetton Railway, and shunting it on to

the staithes and railway sidings for onward transportation. One of the Seaham engines, *Milo*, was photographed in action on 21 July of that year; she was an inside-cylinder 0-6-0T long-boilered engine built for the North Eastern Railway, with that company's numbers 972 and 1662. Note also examples of NER coal wagons and the 4-ton chauldron waggons behind the engine.

Above right Also working at Seaham on that day was 0-6-0 long-boiler tender engine *Clio*, built by Hopkins Gilkes in 1861 for the North Eastern Railway as No 125. Again, 4-ton chauldron waggons can be seen in the picture, as can various members of the train crew.

Right Working for the Londonderry Railway and at times in the Seaham Harbour area was diminutive locomotive No 18. She was built by Lewin in the Dorset Foundry at Poole in 1877 and went new to the Londonderry Railway. She then went to the Seaham Harbour Dock Company in 1899. As can be seen by the comparative size of footplatemen and engine, No 18 really was tiny, with cylinders of only 9 by 18 inches; the sharply inclined cylinders and piston rods were distinguishing features of Lewin's products. She was out of use for many years, then subsequently returned to traffic; when still working in 1966 she became the oldest locomotive in industrial use in the country. A gathering of 4-ton Seaham Harbour Railway chauldron waggons also gives a remarkable scale to a very small engine.

The South Hetton Railway served a number of pits in the south-west part of County Durham and transported the coal to Seaham Harbour for onward distribution. The railway had an amazing collection of locomotives with a variety of histories. In 1933, ten engines worked on the railway in total, and the next five photographs illustrate that variety.

At South Hetton on 20 July 1933, Driver Coulthard poses with an engine with a most interesting history. *Haverhill*, an 0-6-0 outside-cylinder tank, was originally built by Sharp Stewart in 1873, works number 2358, for the Cornwall Mineral Railways, where she was No 10. In 1880 she was sold to the Colne Valley & Halstead Railway in Suffolk, and from there went to South Hetton in 1889. She then worked the remaining 59 years of her life on the South Hetton Railway, being finally withdrawn and broken up on site in 1948.

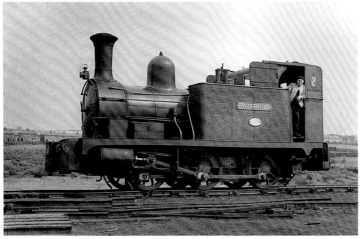

The history of *Sir George* is even more remarkable. She was originally built by Robert Stephenson in 1848 for the Southern division of the London & North Western Railway as LNWR No 216, later 816. She was then sold to the Alexandra Dock Railway, South Wales, in 1875 and named *Sir George Elliot*. Purchased by the South Hetton Colliery in 1895 and renamed *Sir George*, then substantially rebuilt at South Hetton in 1910, she finished her days there after the Second World War and was finally broken up on site in 1953.

Above South Hetton No 6, an outside-cylinder 0-6-0T, was built as a 4-4-0 tank by Beyer Peacock in 1864 (works number 425) for the Metropolitan Railway. She was sold as a 4-4-0 to South Hetton in 1906, only to be rebuilt as an 0-6-0 in 1909. Photographed at South Hetton on 20 July 1933, she was withdrawn and broken up on site in 1948.

Below Inevitably there are some locomotives where a doubt exists over the initial part of their lives. This is particularly so in the case of *Whitfield*, photographed at South Hetton in July 1933. She was certainly built by Sharp Stewart in 1866, works number 1677, for the London & North Western Railway as a six-coupled tender engine. Later she was sold to the West Somerset Mineral Railway and named *Atlas*. Then it is likely she was sold on to the Chatterley Whitfield Railway in Staffordshire, where the name *Whitfield* came about. It is known that she was rebuilt at Ebbw Vale in 1904, presumably as the 0-6-0 long-boilered tank engine that went to South Hetton in 1907. She remained working at South Hetton until the end of the Second World War and was broken up on site in 1948.

In 1973 South Hetton provided the last place in North East England where a steam locomotive could be seen in regular use. Diesels subsequently replaced steam, but with the run-down of the collieries in the area South Hetton shed closed in 1987.

Above Here is a fine example of one of the locomotives actually built in the Lambton engine works at Philadelphia. No 25, an inside-cylinder 0-6-0 tender engine, was constructed there in 1890 and spent all her life on the one system. She had magnificently clocked up 70 years when withdrawn in May 1960.

Below LH&J No 55 is a good example of a locomotive that was built for a specific main-line company, then, at the end of her useful life there, was sold to an

industrial line for a further 28 years' work. This 0-6-2T was built by Kitson in 1887, works number 3069, for the Cardiff Railway, where she was No 28, later becoming No 159 after the grouping as part of Great Western stock. In 1931 she was sold to the Lambton, Hetton & Joicey Company based at Philadelphia. After the nationalisation of 1947, No 55 received a new cab and bunker and a new livery of black with red lining and gold lettering shaded red. She was withdrawn from traffic in October 1959.

Above An interesting railway that served the Durham coalfield was the Pontop & Jarrow. This was one of the largest private railways in the county and came into existence in 1863 through the merger of older collieries' railways. It served the area around Springwell and Marley Hill, and at both of these locations there was an engine shed. Coal was moved over the Pontop & Jarrow Railway to the River Tyne at Jarrow, where there were staithes to allow transfer to ship, and much of the system was worked by gravity and rope haulage. Due mainly to the economic depression of the late 1920s, some of the pits on the line were closed and a new company was formed; from 1932 the complex became known as the Bowes Railway.

One of the engines to work on the line was No 9; an 0-6-0 inside-cylinder long-boilered engine, details of her origins are unknown. What is known is that she

was delivered to the railway in 1860, rebuilt in 1867 and in 1894 at Robert Stephenson's, then again in 1914 by Hawthorn Leslie, and finally by Ridley Shaw of Middlesbrough in 1927. She was broken up in February 1935.

Below Over the river in Northumberland, a visit was paid to Backworth Colliery on 17 July 1933. Astonishingly, of the 15 or so locomotives working at Backworth on that date, nine had all been built in the 1870s and for the North Eastern Railway. With both Backworth Colliery privately owned standard coal wagons and a sample of the 3-ton chauldron waggons in the picture, the ex-North Eastern engine seen here is No 7. She was built by R. W. Hawthorn of Newcastle in 1876, works number 1671, and while on the NER was their No 1364.

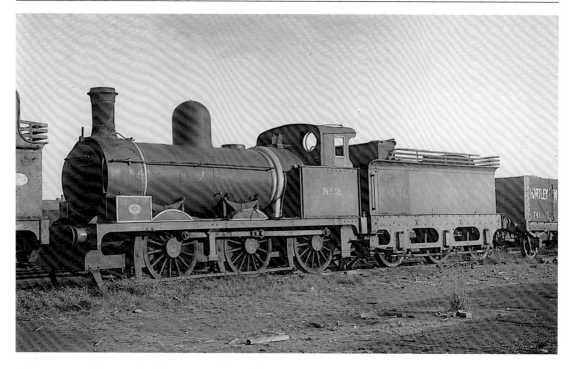

These three photographs show interesting engines that worked at the Hartley Main Coal Company in Northumberland. Coal from this company's collieries were transported by rail to the staithes at Blyth.

Seen at Seaton Delaval on 17 July 1933 is Hartley Main No 2, an inside-cylinder 0-6-0 tender engine; built by Hawthorn in 1867, at some stage she has acquired an ex-GNR Stirling tender.

Also at Seaton Delaval on the same day is No 3, a long-boilered outside-framed 0-6-0 tender engine. Built by Stephenson in 1867, works number 1747, she was initially with the North Eastern Railway as No 658.

Finally, at work at Cramlington on 22 May 1934 is a 2-6-0 outside-cylinder tender engine, Hartley Main No 16, built by Beyer Peacock in 1895, works number 3679, for the Midland & South West Junction Railway as its No 14. Good examples of North Eastern signals worked from Cramlington signal box can be seen behind the tender. Also in the picture are Hartley Main Colliery grease-axlebox coal wagons.

7. Scotland

The Highland Railway conjures up scenes of a most important line, yet much of it single with passing loops and with locomotives and men being called upon to perform heroic feats amongst the snow and the grandeur of the mountains. This is how Dad saw it. He would often visit the important centres of Perth, Aviemore and Inverness, but it was around Dunkeld and the Pass of Killiecrankie that held a special place in his heart. We will start at the southern end and work northwards.

Following the success of the 'Jones Goods' 4-6-0, the first locomotive of this wheel arrangement in Britain, Peter Drummond used the design to build his 'Castles', which were to become the mainstay of express passenger duties over the Highland line.

Nineteen were built between 1900 and 1917, of which the first 16 had 5ft 9in driving wheels and the last three 6ft 0in. After the grouping they became LMS Nos 14675-93. So successful were these engines in Scotland that a further 50, with slight modifications, were built in 1908 by the North British Locomotive Company for the Northern Railway of France.

The lines of the 'Castles' can be seen to advantage on No 14680 *Duncraig Castle*, originally HR No 149, standing on Perth shed on 14 April 1933. Typical of many Highland locomotives are the hinged brake pipes at the front end to permit snow plough attachment. The last of the class was No 14690 *Dalcross Castle*, which remained in service until 1947.

The Pickersgill 4-4-0s were fine locomotives, being an enlargement of McIntosh's well-known 'Dunalastairs'. They all had 6ft 6in driving wheels and a total of 48 were built between 1916 and 1922 at the works of the North British Locomotive Company. No 14501, also seen at Perth on 21 May 1934, was originally Caledonian Railway No 70 and built in 1922. Most of the class were still doing useful work up to 1959, but were then withdrawn very quickly, with the final engine going in 1963.

Photographed in the Killiecrankie area is an up Inverness-Perth express double-headed by a 'Castle' 4-6-0 as train engine and a 'Small Ben' 4-4-0 as leading locomotive. There were 20 'Small Bens' altogether, built to a Drummond design by Dubs, the North British Locomotive Company and at the Highland Railway's own works at Lochgorm (Inverness). In fact, the nine built at Lochgorm were the final tender engines to be built there. They appeared between 1898 and 1906 and subsequently some were rebuilt with Caledonian boilers while others had eight-wheel 'watercart' tenders. Many of the class worked north of Inverness and remained in service into the early 1950s.

Above With a clerestory set, including a Brake next to the tender, one of the ill-fated 'River' 4-6-0s eases through lowland hills towards Killiecrankie with an HR express in 1933 – burn marks on the smokebox door suggest that the engine has been working hard. With Walschaerts valve gear and 6ft 0in driving wheels, the six 'Rivers', built by Hawthorn Leslie in 1915, were designed by Smith to cope with increasing wartime traffic over the Highland line. Well documented is the fact that they were banned from the HR by the Civil Engineer for weight reasons. The tragedy then unfolds that, having sold six excellent engines to the Caledonian Railway, the HR subsequently found that the bridge stress calculations had been unnecessarily severe and the 'Rivers' were allowed to return to the Highland in 1927, which was not before Smith had resigned.

Above right The stone portal of the north end of Killiecrankie Tunnel frames a down freight in 1933. 'Jones Goods' 4-6-0 No 17917 has filled the tunnel with smoke and emerges into the daylight to allow the photographer little time to act. As well as the first 4-6-0s in Britain, these locomotives were also the most powerful main-line engines in the country when built. There were 15 in all, built by Sharp Stewart in 1894 as Highland Railway Nos 103-17; they subsequently became Nos 17916-30 after the grouping.

They were built with flangeless centre driving wheels, but later small flanges were added. Also, in order to improve draught and, consequently, steaming, they received fluted chimneys and wing plates. No 17917 (originally HR No 104) has changed little in her 39 years except for the removal of the wing plates. The class was gradually taken out of service between 1929 and 1940, but the original locomotive, No 103, is preserved.

Right Light work for a large engine! A down local stopping train leaves Killiecrankie Tunnel in 1933 behind Cummings 'Clan' No 14768 *Clan Mackenzie*, running here with a six-wheeled tender. She was originally HR No 56, and was withdrawn from service in 1946.

The mountains look well and form an ideal background to a 'Clan' on a Perth-Inverness stopping train in 1933. The engine this time is No 14763 *Clan Fraser* with a train of Highland stock and a horsebox next to the tender. Behind the train is Killiecrankie station with the appropriate HR signals; an up train, which has been crossed in the platform, is ready to depart southbound. No 14763 was originally HR No 51, and was withdrawn in 1944.

Top A Drummond 4-4-0 of the 'Small Ben' Class prepares for her next duty at Aviemore in 1935. With a tender full of coal and the cab door hinged back, so typical of Highland locomotives, No 14404 *Ben Clebrig* makes ready to work to Forres over Dava. As one of a class of 20, she was built by Dubs in 1899 as HR No 8. She became the last 'Small Ben' in service, lasting into BR days, and latterly her home depot was Wick.

Middle With the Craigellachie nature reserve rather dominant behind, the imposing lines of the 'Clans' are seen to advantage in this shot of No 14764 *Clan Munro* at Aviemore; she was built by Hawthorn Leslie in 1919 as HR No 52. The 'Clans' were gradually taken out of service from 1943, but *Clan Munro* was the last but one to be withdrawn in 1948, an Aviemore engine at the end of her life.

Bottom With her days severely numbered, Highland Railway 4-4-0 No 14379 *Loch Insh* was photographed at Aviemore, where she was based, in 1948. Built by Dubs & Company in 1896, she was HR No 119, and in the 1920s received a Caledonian 'Dunalastair IV' boiler. Aviemore signal box is in the left background.

Left The 'Big Bens' were 4-4-0 passenger engines built for the Highland Railway by the North British Locomotive Company. There were only six in the class and they had a larger boiler and higher pressure than the more successful 'Small Bens'. All had eight-wheeled tenders and had been withdrawn prior to 1939. This example is No 14417 *Ben na Caillach*.

Below The differences between the two classes of 'Ben' 4-4-0s are highlighted in this picture of 'Small Ben' No 14397 *Ben-y-Gloe* taken at Inverness in 1934. She was built for Peter Drummond by Dubs & Company in 1898 and was, in fact, Highland Railway No 1. These engines frequently worked the local stopping trains to the north and east of Inverness.

Left 0-4-2 tank No 15001 was originally built by Dugald Drummond at St Rollox in 1885 for the Caledonian Railway's Killin branch, where she worked until 1895; she was then displaced by the Caley 0-4-4 tanks. After further light duties, she went to Inverness to work the harbour and canal basin branches. She is seen at the wonderful Highland roundhouse at Inverness on 16 April 1933.

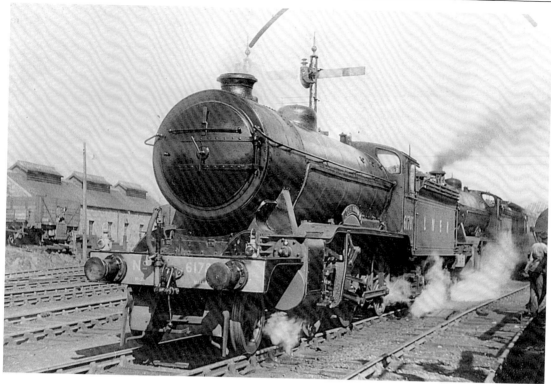

Above Over on the West Highland Extension line just after the Second World War, with Mallaig shed and a lovely NB signal in the background, two ex-Great Northern 'K2' 2-6-0s prepare to leave the fishing port with an express for Fort William and Glasgow Queen Street in 1947. Seventy-five 'K2s' were built by Gresley for the Great Northern between 1912 and 1921, and 13 were rebuilt with cut-down boiler mountings and side-window cabs for working over the West Highland lines. On being transferred, they were named after Scottish lochs, and the picture shows No 61787 *Loch Quoich* and a sister engine looking very smart in their apple green livery. The driver of the leading engine is Harry Cairns, a Mallaig driver with whom Dad became friendly during his various trips to the line.

Below The Great North of Scotland Railway, with a locomotive works at Inverurie from 1902, covered much of rural Aberdeenshire. This included the main line to Keith and Elgin and a number of long branches to Boat of Garten, Banff, Macduff, Peterhead, Fraserburgh and Ballater. To cope with this rural and widespread network, all of the work, both passenger and freight, was performed by 4-4-0 locomotives. Of these, the first were the 'D41s' built by Pickersgill to an 1895 design; there were 39 of them, recognisable by the lack of side-window cabs. No 2240, seen here, was originally GNoS No 96, then 6896 under the LNER scheme and 2240 under BR in 1948. The 'NE' on the tender was very much a wartime arrangement.

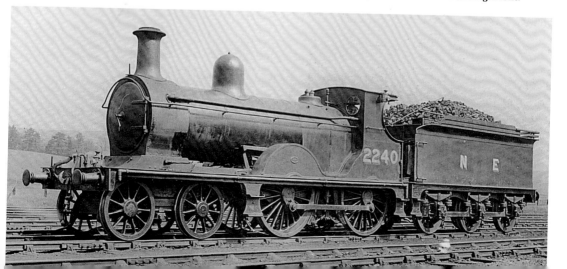

Making rather heavy weather of starting an express freight out of Aberdeen with a cattle wagon next to the engine and surrounded by a veritable forest of GNoS signals is later 4-4-0 Class 'D40' No 2267. The 'D40s' were the former GNoS 'V' Class, built by Neilson in 1899 to a Pickersgill design; they were followed by seven more, which were named in 1920 and superheated while Heywood was Locomotive Superintendent. They were fitted with side-window cabs and, in this case, a tender-cab, making it a far more comfortable ride for the driver and his mate, particularly in winter.

The introduction of the 'B17' three-cylinder 'Sandringham' 4-6-0s to the Great Eastern enabled the release of a number of GER 'B12' 4-6-0s to work elsewhere, and these were sent to Scotland to work on the GNoS section where axle-loading limitations had always been a problem. Compared with the 'D40'/'D41' 4-4-0s, Scottish firemen found that on the 'B12' coal had to be shifted a long way from shovelling plate to firehole door, which earned these engines their 'Hiker' nickname. However, with increasing traffic it was something of a bonus for GNoS operators to have an engine of this capacity working for them.

There were originally 80 'B12' 4-6-0s designed by S. D. Holden for the Great Eastern; they had 6ft 6in driving wheels and some were subsequently rebuilt by Gresley with a larger boiler, but none of these went to the GNoS. The first 'B12' went to the Great North of Scotland Railway system in 1926 to participate in loading tests on bridges, and subsequently 20 went to Kittybrewster between 1931 and 1939. No 1524, painted in LNER green, is seen leaving Inverurie with an Aberdeen to Inverness express. Note on the platform a feature linked with water columns – a coal-fired brazier to protect the water from frost.

Index of locations